UNDERSTANDING

Autistic

BEHAVIORS

Improving Health,
Independence and Well-being

Book Two in the Understanding Autism Series

THERESA M. REGAN, PHD, CAS

Neuropsychologist & Certified Autism Specialist

indiego | **PUBLISHING**
Our Brilliance . Your Success

Paperback ISBN 9781946824141
Hardcover ISBN 9781946824158
Ebook ISBN 9781946824165
LCCN: 2018932678

Published in the United States of America
INDIEGO PUBLISHING LLC
www.indiegopublishing.com

Publisher's Cataloging-In-Publication Data:
Names: Regan, Theresa M.
Title: Understanding autistic behaviors : improving health, independence, and well-being / Theresa M. Regan, Ph.D., CAS, Neuropsychologist, Certified Autism Specialist.
Description: [Deltona, Florida] : IndieGo Publishing LLC, [2018]
Identifiers: ISBN 9781946824141 (paperback) | ISBN 9781946824158 (hardback) | ISBN 9781946824165 (ebook)
Subjects: LCSH: Autism spectrum disorders--Treatment--Popular works. | Autism spectrum disorders in children--Treatment--Popular works. | Autistic people--Care--Popular works.
Classification: LCC RC553.A88 R442 2018 (print) | LCC RC553.A88 (ebook) | DDC 616.85882--dc23

Other Books
by Theresa Regan:

Understanding Autism in Adults and Aging Adults 1ˢᵗ and 2ⁿᵈ Editions
2017 Best Book Awards Finalist in the Health:
Aging/50+ category

Soul Cries
2013 National Indie Excellence Award Finalist

Learn more at the author's website:
www.adultandgeriatricautism.com

Table of Contents

Introduction

Setting the Stage

*A*utism spectrum disorder (ASD) is a developmental, neurologic condition present across the lifespan. What does that mean? To put it simply, ASD is present in early childhood development, involves brain function, and persists in some form throughout adolescence and adulthood, even as the individual progresses through the aging process. ASD is not a disorder of intellect, although it can be present in individuals who also have an intellectual disability. Rather, autism is broadly characterized as a condition of behavior, communication, and social connections.

As outlined in detail in my book *Understanding Autism in Adults and Aging Adults 2nd Edition*, the diagnostic criteria for ASD include symptoms of social communication and relationships, repetitive behaviors, rigid thought processes, fixed interests or strong attachment to objects, as well as sensory processing challenges, such as over- or under-reactivity to the sensory environment or fixation on certain sensory experiences.

In addition to the core diagnostic criteria, there are many commonly associated symptoms of ASD, such as sleep disturbance, dyspraxia (problems with coordinated movements to produce meaningful activities), uneven cognitive and learning profiles, inattention, and difficulties with the regulation of emotions and behavior.

This book will not attempt to discuss autism spectrum disorder as a diagnosis, nor will it outline what the condition may look like across the lifespan. (For this discussion, please refer to *Understanding Autism in Adults and Aging Adults 2nd Edition*.) This book is designed to increase your understanding of autistic behaviors and to help you develop interventions to support better behavioral outcomes in the ASD individual in your family, your circle of friends, your classroom, or in your care.

Many books have been written about the autism spectrum, so why write a book about behaviors in particular? In my experience, patients and families seek help from their local autism clinic because they want to see behavioral change at home. Often they have tried a number of tactics and feel that they have fallen short. Frequently they are frustrated and in need of immediate practical solutions to achieve a happier outcome for everyone involved.

What do we mean by behavioral change? This may include increasing positive life-affirming behaviors such as interacting with others or looking for a job that is well suited to the individual. Behavioral change may also include decreasing problematic behaviors such as escape behaviors (spending much of the day isolated, or leaving town when stressed), repetitive behaviors (pacing or hand-washing), or outbursts (meltdowns or aggressive behaviors). Some individuals see many psychiatrists for medication advice on behavior management before considering routines, structured settings, guidelines, and other practical options that can be implemented in daily life. The search for a medication solution is often frustrating. Although medication can be a layer of support for the individual in the spectrum, it should be viewed as one piece of the behavioral puzzle rather than the only, or even primary, solution to achieving a sense of well-being in the autistic individual. Focusing on behavioral change strategies is also key to improving the individual's quality of life and overall health.

In utilizing this book, you can expect to:

- Receive an introduction to the concepts underlying brain-behavior relationships, or how an individual's brain and behaviors are linked.
- Recognize common behavioral symptoms, concerns, and patterns within the autism spectrum.
- Develop an understanding of basic intervention concepts to improve outcomes such as health, safety, calmness, communication, and task completion.

One of the quickest avenues to discouragement in seeking behavioral change is to start the journey with misunderstandings of what a good outcome will look like. In that vein, this book will **not** attempt to do the following:

This book will **not** suggest that behavioral strategies will completely remove challenging behaviors and patterns for the individual in the autistic spectrum. After all, ASD in and of itself is a condition of neurologically based behavioral patterns. Behavioral symptoms will likely persist in some form and to varying degrees across the seasons of life, from childhood to young adulthood to middle age to senior adulthood. For a comparison, think about parenting techniques. Just because you are using great parenting tools does not mean your two-year-old will never have a meltdown in a crowded mall. Your child will still be a child no matter how skilled you are at parenting, but if you know and apply some effective parenting techniques, you can avoid those meltdowns as much as possible.

Likewise, the techniques in this book are offered to help reduce problematic interactions, improve health and safety, and bring about better outcomes in the course of daily living. Overall, when the strategies in this book are consistently implemented across the lifespan, you can realistically expect to see improvements in autistic behavioral patterns.

At the same time, however, behavioral strategies do not change the innate tendencies of the autistic brain that led to a diagnosis of ASD in the first place. The behavioral strategies presented in this book are a way to manage a chronic condition more effectively.

This book does **not** offer a comprehensive and detailed explanation of all the neuro-anatomical ways the brain affects emotions and behavior. Rather, this text will help support your understanding of how the brain impacts the ways in which behaviors manifest themselves in daily life.

This book does **not** outline every possible behavioral concern and intervention approach. However, it does offer general topics with examples and activities to help you apply these in practical ways. These opportunities to practice concepts will stimulate creative thinking as you formulate ideas and action plans to support behavior change with the ASD individual in your care, and to use an "informed trial-and-error approach" to see what works for the particular individual with whom you are interacting.

The most common question I am asked after providing education to patients and families about the diagnosis of ASD is, "What do we do now?" Without a practical, workable action plan, parents and caregivers feel bereft of solutions and alone in their struggle, as if it's up to them to figure out how to make this work for everyone involved. This book is where our understanding of autism becomes useful and meaningful, and as a result, improves everyday life for the ASD individual and his or her caretakers, health providers, instructors, family members, and friends. When we correctly interpret the behaviors of the ASD individual, we can support his or her strengths while diminishing struggles in the areas of health, safety, independent functioning, and relationships.

Chapter 1

Understanding the Brain-Behavior Link

*H*istorically, the realization that some individuals are unable to learn certain life and work skills even with extra instruction and training emerged in the 1800s. Although for many years this diagnosis was referred to as mental retardation, clinicians now use the term intellectual disability (ID). Indeed, the needs of individuals with ID have become well- integrated into formal policies and community programs. In comparison, however, there remains a significant lack of understanding that, in addition to neurologic conditions of intellect, there are also neurologic conditions of behavior. One such condition is developmental and is called autism spectrum disorder (ASD).

In a related string of thought, the late 1800s and early 1900s saw breakthroughs in the understanding of biology and genetics. For example, it became scientifically apparent that parents pass on certain characteristics to their offspring. This understanding became the basis for movements such as social Darwinism and eugenics, which had an impact on immigration and other policies during that period.

Understandably, in response to the destructive thoughts and policies that were instrumental in WWII, public opinion changed from emphasizing genetics ("nature") to emphasizing environment ("nurture") as being of primary importance in personal outcomes. Today, remnants of the strong emphasis on the impact of environment, motivation, and personal character as being of primary or sole impact on personal outcomes echo through topics of parenting and education, and in various community policies. This emphasis brings with it the suggestion that anything is possible if you work hard enough—a worldview that is not actually true—and carries additional baggage that hinders our complete understanding of biological influences on behavior.

Consider the following scenarios:

- The mother of a ten-month-old boy is told that his crying "disrupts the class" at infant daycare. She is asked to "fix him" before bringing him back to the program. Is she a bad mother?

- A twenty-seven-year-old young man who graduated high school without becoming a functional reader is driving a school bus to make ends meet because that's the only job he can find. He feels guilt and shame for his inability to master reading and to understand basic academic concepts. Did he not work hard enough while he was in school?

- A fourteen-year-old girl explodes when she is jostled in the bus line moments after learning that her usual bus monitor is out sick and has been replaced by a new person. The school tells her parents that this explosion is "one too many," and her "erratic behavior and noncompliance with rules and authority" gives them no choice but to suggest a residential behavior program to "teach her the consequences of her bad behavior." The school administrators also recommend that the girl's mother and stepfather take parenting classes. Is the girl "noncompliant" at school? Are her parents lax about teaching behavioral boundaries at home?

The most difficult aspect of understanding challenging behavior is that the nature versus nurture question has no clear categorical answer. Neither genetics and biology nor environment and motivation are solely responsible for behavioral outcomes. It is sometimes baffling to consider the complexity of how one's inherent nature and one's environment impact expressions of emotion, thought, and behavioral regulation. In truth, we all have a biological substrate, an area of boundary from which we cannot deviate. It is from within our biological starting point that we can impact and influence our environment and behavior, but we cannot achieve behaviors that are beyond the capacity of how our brain is "wired" uniquely and individually for each of us.

Consider these examples of biological starting points:

- Because of the parameters of my genes, I will grow within a certain range of height. Certain environmental factors can influence my final height including deficiencies in childhood nutrition and variations in growth hormones. However, it is not true that I can become ten feet tall just because I have good character and strong motivation.

- We each have influence over many aspects of our health, but we cannot entirely prevent every disease or physical problem in our bodies. Many times, we do everything we can and still have physical problems such as arthritis, organ failure, and cancers. We start with a physical body, we do what we can to live a healthy life, but in the end, we cannot live entirely outside the limitations of our genetics.

- A two-year-old is able to learn many things in normal development. She is taking in huge amounts of new information every day. However, if I ask her to sit down at a desk and learn nuclear physics, I have taken her beyond what her brain is capable of doing. Her failure to learn the material is not a result of noncompliance, poor motivation, or lack of effort. She does not lack character because she won't sit still "and at least try." She is working within her biology and is learning what she can accomplish at that age of development.

Getting back to the context of this book—autistic behaviors across the lifespan—while it is not true that the ASD individual has behaviors that are predetermined and unchangeable, it is also not true that he can show complete, flexible, and consistent control over his behaviors at all times. Nor is it true that explaining why he should behave differently—relying on reasoning, facts, and encouragement—will produce the lasting change we hope to see even when he puts forth his best effort.

Think again about the example of height. You could repeatedly explain to me that if I were taller I could reach the top shelf in the kitchen cabinets, but this doesn't mean that I can become taller by good intentions and effort. Rather than cycling through repeated discussions about why change is important, the ASD individual will require strategies and specific supports that fit her own individual strengths and challenges.

We all live within the constraints of certain limitations and areas of influence. To the extent to which our goal is to positively influence behaviors and emotional regulation, we must understand what the limits and influences are for an ASD individual in his or her particular season of life. Never start working toward behavioral change outside the boundary of what the individual is capable of doing at that time. Limits and abilities are unique to the individual and should be understood as clearly as possible before undergoing an effort toward behavioral change.

In the same way that I will not ask a two-year-old to be a nuclear physicist, I will not ask you to accomplish behavioral goals you are not capable of reaching at this time. To do so would be to set the stage for failure, frustration, anxiety, and shame. You would essentially experience failure and sometimes punishment as well (e.g., "If you aren't a nuclear physicist by the end of the year, the consequence will be…").

Instead, I will be a detective to figure out what your strengths and challenges are. I will help you make positive changes by asking you to do something within your range of abilities and with appropriate support. I will use strategies to make the expected behavioral outcomes attainable and practical. The interventions will be strategy-based with the specific ASD individual in mind.

Let's set the stage with a list of terms we will return to again and again in this book:

Detective

I invite you to consider yourself a detective rather than a police officer as you discover workable methods to bring about positive behavioral change with the ASD individual in your life. Understand that all behavior is communication. When you see a certain behavior in someone, consider that it reveals the internal state and capacities of the individual at that time. Gather information about what behaviors you see, when they occur, and in what environments. You are not here to police others' behavior. Instead, you are a detective on a fact-finding mission. Welcome to your new role. Fact-finding is the first step toward strategic behavioral interventions.

Strategies

Next, I invite you to always think strategically in response to behavior. Again, you are not a police officer. You have gathered information as a detective. You understand that the behavior reflects the individual's internal state. Can you put the pieces together to make strategies for intervention? Approach the goal of behavior change with a strategic mindset rather than a mindset of complaint, impatience, policing, or shaming. You are a detective who interacts strategically with the individual to produce positive change and to improve both internal comfort and external behaviors.

Self-Regulation

You will see the word "regulation" quite a bit in this book. To regulate is to manage the strength, speed, or flow of something. A regulator may increase or decrease a particular quality of something, such as to regulate the temperature of a room, the flow of a river, or the rate of metabolism. Something that is regulated is kept at an even keel, kept in check, kept at a level that is healthy and comfortable.

When we talk about behavioral symptoms, we are pointing out areas in which the individual lacks appropriate behavioral or emotional regulation. Typically, our brains should be effective at understanding the state of the body, regulating emotional and physical experiences accordingly, and expressing behaviors that are calm, effective, safe, and healthy. Someone who struggles with self-regulation is said to be emotionally or behaviorally dysregulated.

Over-Reactive

If there is one state that an autistic may lean toward, it is the state of feeling overwhelmed by her external and/or internal environment. Many individuals in the spectrum describe the world as feeling too intense. Synonyms for "overwhelmed" include swamped, buried, deluged, flooded, or inundated. The word can be used to suggest that someone is defeated by an opponent, routed, conquered, or overcome. Someone may feel overwhelmed when they are given too much, as in being inundated with input. The brain of the ASD individual does not process information and stimuli efficiently enough to prevent a feeling of inundation from incoming messages. Individuals with ASD may be overwhelmed by memories, details, emotions, and sensations. The intensity of the world can lead to an overwhelmed state that manifests in dysregulated behavior. The individual may behave in an over-reactive manner to qualities of the environment that neurotypical people consider common or normative (e.g., criticism from others, loud noises).

Dysregulated Behavior

Many people mistakenly think that dysregulated behavior only manifests as an outburst or meltdown, but this is not the case. There are three variations in behavioral responses in which dysregulation can be present:

- **Fight**. Fight responses signal the presence of an overwhelmed state. This is perhaps the most recognizable category to observers. The autistic individual who is overwhelmed by change may react in a fight pattern; as an example, he shouts and has an explosive episode when his physician's office calls unexpectedly to cancel a scheduled appointment. An ASD individual who feels trapped on a school bus because of too much noise, the close presence of other raucous students, and the ups and downs of hills on the road may seem to "snap" by shouting and pushing people away. These fight responses are often defensive in nature, an effort to "push away" the offending stimuli, to make the world stop its invading inputs.

- **Flight**. Perhaps a less frequently noticed response to environmental intensity is a flight response. A person may figuratively "fly away" from an overwhelming work situation—being corrected by a supervisor, feeling pressured to meet a deadline, told to participate in a meeting—by walking out and going home rather than staying at work to finish his shift.

  Another ASD individual may show flight when she puts the bed covers over her head while her husband is talking to her about a difficult topic. These are considered flight responses because they exemplify the urge to escape a situation that feels overwhelming.

- **Freeze**. The autistic may also "freeze" all behaviors as a coping mechanism and even appear catatonic, such as sitting and staring for an hour without responding to the questions of family members. Another may talk to himself and rock forward and backward when he learns that his dog has passed away, for example. This freezing behavior has a "stuck" quality because the person lacks appropriate interaction with the environment, and sometimes seems immersed in his own internal world.

Although each of these types of behaviors may be seen in one individual, it may also be that the individual leans toward one or two categories of dysregulation more than to others. One individual may be prone to outbursts while another exhibits escaping and freezing behaviors.

Although these reactive behaviors can be seen in all individuals, whether in the spectrum or not, this tendency toward dysregulation is much more noticeable in the autistic individual than in his or her neurotypical peers.

Under-Reactive

In contrast to the over-reactive individual who experiences the world as intense and therefore seeks ways to stop the intensity by fight, flight, or freeze reactions, there are under-reactive ASD individuals whose lack of awareness or reaction to the environment produces a different set of behaviors. Being under-reactive is common in autism and may be seen in the individual who appears disinterested, passive, or disengaged from what is happening around her. In this case, she is not overwhelmed because of heightened awareness. Instead, she is under-aware of what is going on in her environment. She is apt to miss information from the environment and to experience the world as under-whelming, too subtle, and not compelling in any significant way. She may seem "spaced out" or in her own world.

In contrast to the individual who freezes in an intense environment, the under-reactive individual misses important information, such as being unaware of pain during a medical emergency and thus not calling his doctor, or when he misses other sensory cues that should prompt him to bathe, brush his teeth, eat on a regular basis, drink water, and wear clean clothes. The under-reactive individual misses social cues and lacks a response to the environment that typically would compel an individual to meet goals and fully engage in life.

It should be noted that a combination of over-reactivity and under-reactivity can be seen in the same ASD individual. Sometimes this is sensory specific—the individual may over-react to touch and under-react to sound. There may also be variability across times of day and days or weeks. Many autistics describe that they have varying experiences over the course of time, and may share comments such as, "I know what kind of day I'm having when I try to brush my teeth but I can't because it hurts or annoys me, or it makes me gag." They may describe having had a rough couple of months before feeling better regulated for reasons that are hard to pin down.

For those who observe the ASD individual's behavior and find this dynamic of over- and under-reactivity confusing, especially when considered in tandem with the variety of symptoms that manifest over time (sometimes seemingly disparate symptoms), let's consider some comparisons.

Pregnancy may be one such example. When I was pregnant, my sense of smell was greatly heightened and led to quite a bit of nausea and avoidance of certain environments. It was amazing to me that a simple hormonal change meant that my brain had this heightened reaction to even "nice" smells such as flowers, foods that I typically enjoy, and soap. These were now strongly aversive to me. By the middle of my second trimester, my hormones changed again, and my smell aversions were gone. I experienced a season of over-reactivity and then a change back to my baseline state because of a hormone change. This experience helped me understand that biology itself can lead to variations in how one experiences and reacts to the world.

Another comparison may be the experiences of those who become intoxicated from alcohol and then are hung over after a night of drinking. We know that the state of intoxication occurs because alcohol impacts brain function. The individual who is intoxicated shows imbalance while walking, says and does things she ordinarily wouldn't say or do, makes unsafe decisions, slurs her speech, and has amnesia for portions of events. The next morning, she complains that lights are too bright and sounds are too loud, and the slightest movement makes her feel like she's spinning. These changes in sensation and behavior are related to the physiological impact that alcohol has on brain function. The experience of being hung over from alcohol is yet another common example of how changes in biology can change the way an individual experiences and reacts to his or her environment.

Changes within the brain lead to changes in the way we experience the world, behave, think, and make decisions. Realizing that the autistic's dysregulated behaviors and unusual reactions are biologically based (although not fully determined), and are related to how he or she experiences the environment is an important part of understanding brain-behavior relationships. This understanding can be used to work more effectively toward comfort and improved regulation of behavior for each autistic individual.

In this chapter, we have laid significant groundwork for our journey toward behavioral change. We have learned that behavior has a seat in the brain and therefore shows some inherent boundaries and limitations. We understand that humans have influence, although not complete and consistent control over the expression of behaviors and emotions. We have put aside our typical roles as police officers who dole out correction, call for compliance, and point out the various ways that people fall short of the rules. Instead, we have accepted the role of detective to gather information while understanding that all behavior is a form of communication that reveals important information about the individual's internal state and reactions to the environment. We have learned to recognize when an ASD individual is over- or underwhelmed (over- or under-reactive), and we have embraced a commitment to use strategy-based interventions toward better outcomes.

Lastly, we have learned that behaviors that are rooted in brain function will show changes over time and be expressed differently across seasons of life and varying environments. We now understand that erratic, inconsistent, and unusual behaviors are not in themselves evidence of any willfulness or lack of motivation to change. At the same time, we understand that there are behavioral strategies that will help the ASD individual feel more engaged, comfortable, and productive.

To help you embrace the information presented in this book, I will be inviting you to participate in practice exercises. These exercises may provide hypothetical examples, opportunities to brainstorm strategies, and space for you to list your own examples relevant to the concepts discussed in each chapter. You may use any system of note taking that works best for you if you prefer not to write your responses in the book.

The behavioral concepts described in this chapter are listed below followed by an example of each concept. Take some time to practice your understanding of the concepts.

Practice the Concepts Learned

"Police officer" vs. "Detective"

What might a "police officer" say in response to a preteen who is fidgety at dinner? He kicks his feet against his chair, gets up frequently, and bangs his fork against the plate.

> "If you can't sit still at the dinner table, you'll have to go to your room without supper."

What might a "detective" say in response to this behavior?

> "I see your body is full of energy tonight. How can we help you feel better and still be able to eat dinner with the family?"

Here are more examples of behaviors. Take a moment to write down the differences between what a police officer and a detective might say in response to the behaviors as demonstrated above.

Example 1: A sixty-year-old ASD gentleman walks out of his doctor's office during a discussion about changing his diet to avoid salt and cholesterol.

A "police officer might do the following:

_____

_____

_____

_____

_____

A "detective" might do the following:

_____

_____

_____

_____

_____

Example 2: A twelve-year-old girl in the spectrum begins crying and pacing after being defeated in a chess competition.

A "police officer" might do the following:

_____

_____

_____

_____

_____

A "detective" might do the following:

_____

_____

_____

_____

Example 3: A young woman stares ahead without responding to her boyfriend, who is frustrated with her refusal to accompany him to a party at his boss's house.

A "police officer" might do the following:

_____

_____

_____

_____

_____

A "detective" might do the following:

_____

_____

_____

_____

_____

Over-reactivity: Fight, Flight, and Freeze

When an autistic individual feels overwhelmed by an intense environment, observers may identify fight, flight, or freeze behaviors. Make a list of what kinds of overwhelmed behaviors may fall into each category. A few examples have been provided for each category. Add some ideas for each category based on your own experiences or by generating hypothetical examples.

Fight

Example 1: An ASD employee yells on the phone at his boss when he is told that his regular work hours are being changed for the next week.

Example 2: An adolescent begins pacing and yelling when her parents repeatedly tell her to clean her room. During the next several hours, she demonstrates no progress toward completing that goal.

Example 3 (write your own):

_____

_____

_____

_____

_____

_____

Flight

Example 1: A seven-year-old comes home from school and curls up under the dining room table rather than engaging with his babysitter.

Example 2: A grandfather retreats to his room when his kids and grandkids come over for Thanksgiving dinner.

Example 3 (write your own):

_____

_____

_____

_____

_____

_____

Freeze

Example 1: A young woman in her twenties is being evaluated for possible seizures related to staring spells during times of stress. The EEG documents no seizure activity, and the spells appear to be a behavioral reaction to stress.

Example 2: An ASD gentleman pulled over by a police officer for running a red light stares at her without speaking. The officer suspects him of being intoxicated because of his apparent confusion and lack of appropriate interaction with her.

Example 3 (write your own):

_____

_____

_____

_____

_____

_____

Under-Reactivity

Write some examples describing the ASD individual who is under-reactive to the environment, meaning s/he fails to notice important information in her surroundings and interactions with others.

Example 1: A sixteen-year-old ASD teen becomes so engrossed when reading about astronomy in the school library that he does not notice or respond to the fire alarm.

Example 2: A thirty-year-old woman with ASD eats and eats without sensing when she is full. This lack of awareness of her internal sensations causes problems with obesity, diabetes, and high blood pressure over her lifespan.

Example 3: A fifty-year-old man in the spectrum is unaware of the filth in his living environment. He does not notice what needs to be cleaned, nor does he keep up with repairs. He also seems unaware of his sister's stress and concern for him because of his lack of progress with improved housekeeping.

Example 4 (write your own):

_____

_____

_____

_____

_____

_____

Chapter 2

The Physics of Behavior

$\mathcal{T}$his chapter explores ways in which the brain affects the expression of emotions and behaviors. The behavioral concepts discussed will be brought to life through analogy with physical laws, thus the "Physics of Behavior." These illustrations, in combination with examples of behaviors seen in individuals in the autism spectrum, will bring meaning to the concepts discussed in this book, and will serve as a springboard for further discussion and problem solving.

The Pull Toward a Behavioral Default

The law of gravity has to do with objects experiencing a "pull toward" the earth. Although we can "defy" gravity during activities in which our feet leave the ground for brief periods when we're jumping or flipping, our default state of being is to feel the pull of the earth's gravity back to the ground.

We can use the analogy of gravity to discuss how behaviors have a default mode as well. Although all humans show variability of behavior, we typically also have a default mode, a behavioral set that we tend toward. Someone may describe you by saying you are "typically" detail-oriented and resistant to change. Although you can likely "defy" your default for short bursts, you will eventually feel the "pull" of the ground, the "tug" back toward your default ways of behaving and experiencing the world.

The same is true for the autistic individual. Although she may be able to put forth effort for short bursts of time to "defy gravity" and deviate from her default, she will feel that biological tug back to her more typical behavioral pattern. For example, the ASD individual who prefers alone time in her room can attend a social gathering or event, and function as expected because she knows there is a definite end to the activity. However, this short burst is an example of defying gravity, and therefore it takes some effort on her part. She will feel a drain on her energy and a pull back to her default state of needing extensive time alone.

Although we can expect her to defy gravity for brief periods, we must understand that the pull toward the default of being alone is strong because this is a brain-based pattern. Additionally, the energy drain she experiences from being in a social setting is likely to appear as a drain in overall resiliency for a certain period afterward. The world may feel even more intense during her recovery period. She may show more fight, flight, or freeze behaviors during this time. The individuals around her who embrace the identity of "detective" rather than "police officer" will see these heightened behavioral responses and understand that they are evidence that she is in a recovery period and feels the drain of defying her default earlier in the day, and possibly even the previous day or the night before.

Although there are things we can do to support her comfort level and confidence when interacting in groups, we would be mistaken to think that just because we observe glimpses of change in her behavioral pattern that she can effortlessly maintain this altered state "if only she tries hard enough or cares deeply enough about everyone else." In other words, the pull toward the default behavioral pattern does not reflect issues of motivation or character. Rather, it reflects this "law of gravity"—the tendency to be pulled back to the ground (her default behavioral norm) after defying gravity for short bursts.

Inertia: Difficulty Switching Behavioral Gears

Newton's first law of motion describes inertia by saying that in order for the motion of an object to change, a force must act upon it. An object at rest tends to stay at rest. An object in motion tends to stay in motion unless a force acts upon it. Likewise, behaviors and behavioral patterns require some form of input, effort, or push to change states. Typically, this input comes from the individual's own brain or from outside influences in the environment.

The center (subcortical) and front of the brain are densely connected. This frontal-subcortical system is problematic in the autism spectrum, and this circuitry significantly impacts behavior. You can think of this brain system as an "ON-OFF" switch in the brain. These areas of brain connection are meant to give the "go or no" signal for behavior. This system is sometimes referred to as the "social screen door" because it helps the person say "no" to certain behaviors, like taking off his shirt when he feels hot at the office, and "go" to other behaviors, like getting up from watching TV to complete his work presentation or to get some exercise.

When functioning normally, this part of the brain helps us get going when we are at rest and stop when we are in motion, thus overcoming our own inertia. The frontal-subcortical system should help us focus on something important, but be able to switch focus and show flexibility of thought and behavior when something else gets our attention that is more important. These brain connections and systems are designed to help us shift from states of inertia as needed—to start moving when at rest and to stop moving when in motion.

Autistic adults find it difficult to shift from activity to inactivity and back again in a way that is productive and meaningful.

Consider the following scenarios:

- A fifty-six-year-old postal worker has always relied on his structured workplace to provide the force he needed to propel him into the activity of getting to work and starting his day after being in a state of rest at home. At work he is given a schedule and told where to be and when. After retirement, his brain has difficulty replacing that external structure, and its rules and deadlines, with an internal push to get up in the morning, take a shower, and complete important household tasks or involve himself in meaningful hobbies and activities.

- A seventy-two-year-old woman began swimming nine years ago and has never missed a single day at the pool. Holidays, illnesses, and road conditions have never hindered her forward "motion" of making her way to the pool to swim laps. Her doctor has asked her to take two weeks away from the pool because she had developed muscle strain and inflammation in her shoulder. Although from a logical perspective she understands that this is wise advice, her brain is inefficient at helping her stop this forward movement toward the pool and to switch gears into rest. Initially she is very uncomfortable and restless about not going to the pool, but after two weeks, she has settled into a state of inertia and is reluctant to return to the pool because now it seems like so much effort to pack her swim gear and go. Now she is in a state of rest, and her brain is not giving her the internal push she needs to get to the pool again. When an individual struggles with shifting from one state of being to another, it can lead to too much of one activity, too little of another activity, and lack of involvement in meaningful activities as situations change.

Behavioral Pushback or Resistance to Change

Newton's third law of motion states that when one object exerts a force on another object, there is an equal and opposite force toward the original object. That is, if you push against a wall, you will feel "pushback" or resistance from the wall.

One of the behaviors I have noticed in ASD individuals is the tendency to push back when external forces try to move them toward change of thought or action. One of the diagnostic characteristics of autism is the presence of rigid and inflexible behaviors. This rigidity may be manifest as strong beliefs, fixed ideas, and stubborn opinions regardless of new information. An example is the categorical thinking that certain things are "good" or "bad" without an age-appropriate appreciation of complexity or an understanding of individual differences. Another manifestation of rigidity may include repetitive patterns of behavior and routines such as arranging the pantry items by color and size, or an insistence that the laundry is done before the kitchen counters are wiped during morning chores. The behaviors in themselves may lack meaningful function—it is not important whether one does laundry or wipes the counters first—or an appreciation of the bigger picture of the situation or interaction.

An individual who works with an autistic person may act as an external force to propel the autistic individual toward change if he does not appear internally motivated to do so. Many autistics react in opposition to this guidance, and say they feel "pushed" by others or "need time" to make decisions and process new information. They exert an opposing force of resistance to what they experience as outside pressure to change.

Consider the following scenarios:

- A sixty-two-year-old autistic gentleman is hospitalized for acute pain in his upper abdomen. His physician wants to conduct some imaging studies to see if his gallbladder is inflamed. The patient resists making any kind of decision about consent for the procedure, but when questioned about his hesitation, he identifies no specific concerns or reasons as to why he feels uncertain. Furthermore, he delays the decision with vague statements such as, "Well, we'll just have to see," or, "I'll have to think about it."

The patient could not identify any new information he needed to make a decision, nor could he pinpoint how his "thinking about it" might lead to a decision. His vague statements seemed to be more of a resistance to change and new ideas than a reasoned response as to why he wouldn't agree to a vital medical procedure.

- A twenty-four-year-old woman complains that she feels "pushed" by her parents to enroll in college or get a job, and to gain some independence. Her equal and opposite reaction to their persuasion is to commence a campaign of stalling, resistance, and indecision.

This kind of significant resistance to change is part of the frontal-subcortical dysfunction that is typical of autism. In other words, the autistic individual is demonstrating behaviors that are expected within the spectrum rather than simply rejecting the advice of others out of stubbornness.

Momentum: The Tendency Toward Behavioral Repetition

In physics, momentum is the property of an object that is moving. Momentum is equal to the product of the object's mass and velocity. In other words, an object gains strength of motion (momentum) based on its size and speed. A semi-truck loaded with construction materials has more momentum and is harder to stop than a bicycle.

Sometimes an ASD individual's behaviors gain momentum and become a "behavioral loop" that the person is drawn into with very little effort and without needing any force to continue, but that requires significant effort to stop. The behavioral pattern has momentum.

This was the case for the elderly hospital patient who had been walking the halls for many hours. Staff called me with concerns because there appeared to be no explanation for the walking. The patient used his walker, but the nursing staff were concerned that he would become fatigued and take a fall. The gentleman was resistant to their requests that he sit down and rest. When I came to see him, we walked the hall together, and he explained that his doctor told him that walking would help relieve his constipation.

In this instance, his doctor's advice had been a push in a certain direction. The behavior gained momentum, and in the context of autism, it easily became something that was harder to stop than to repeat. In other words, it became a repetitive loop.

The autistic brain has a default setting toward repetition. Behaviors, once started, can easily gain momentum and continue over time. This tendency toward repetition and momentum can be very helpful if the behaviors are healthy and safe, but easily problematic if a safer alternative is needed.

Walking to lose weight is healthy. Therefore, an ASD individual who begins a walking program and experiences the development of momentum for this behavior is likely to see improved health. In this example, the momentum of walking happens to create a healthy behavioral pattern for the individual in the spectrum.

In contrast, an autistic individual may show momentum toward a habit that is not healthy, such as eating potato chips for breakfast and hot dogs for lunch and dinner over the course of several years. This particular momentum of an unhealthy behavior becomes a behavioral loop that takes much more force to stop than to continue.

Thirdly, consider the example of an individual with autism who receives instructions from his medical doctor to shower and brush his teeth regularly. This healthy practice takes hold, creating a behavioral loop. However, after he's wounded in a car accident, he demonstrates meltdowns in the hospital when he is not allowed to brush his teeth or take a shower for three days. The stress of not being able to do this "good behavior" is related to the momentum that the behavior has gained over time, even if the individual understands why he can't take a shower or brush his teeth for a few days.

These examples are indicative of how the autistic individual leans toward repetition, which results in a behavioral momentum. Whether the behaviors are healthy or unhealthy, the momentum creates an internal push to continue the behavior, which creates stress in the individual when he is unable to complete the behavioral loop.

Acceleration: Gaining Behavioral Intensity

Acceleration is the rate of change of velocity (speed) as a function of time. Although in physics, slowing down (deceleration) is also a form of acceleration (change in speed), for our purposes we will think of its more common use as the increase of speed over time. The object that is accelerating is increasing in speed. In the case of the ASD individual, one can see a kind of acceleration when a learned behavior gains intensity over time.

Let's consider the ASD individual who started exercising thirty minutes a day, and within six months was exercising two hours every morning and two hours every night. This routine gained momentum and became a repetitive behavior that was difficult to stop, but it also accelerated. In this case, it gradually became more intense and time consuming.

To clarify, we are not stating that it's problematic to have an exercise routine or to do healthy activities on a set schedule. Rather, the problem is when that activity becomes an all-consuming loop that controls the individual with an almost magnetic pull toward repetition for no apparent reason, and infringes on his or her life to a certain degree. Something that is good for you typically has some type of boundary in time (how often you do that thing) and intensity (how much of the activity you do in one setting). Balance is important with any behavior. The autistic can show difficulties with extremes of behavioral patterns, such as too little of a behavior or too frequent or intense a behavior that goes beyond what is healthy or necessary. Not only might an autistic individual lean toward repetition (momentum), but the behaviors can also show a tendency to gain intensity and/or duration (acceleration).

Magnetism: Forces of Behavioral Attraction

Magnetism is a force that pulls certain metals toward the magnet and repels other magnets. If we stick with the analogy between physical forces and brain-behavior connections, we can see some similarities between the concept of magnetism and the presence of "highly restricted, fixated interests that are abnormal in intensity or focus" within the autism spectrum, as specified in the diagnostic criteria of the DSM-5. That is, the individual within the spectrum often feels significantly "pulled" and drawn toward certain topics we may call their "special interests." These can be as varied as drawing, role-playing video games, or physics. These individuals experience a strong attraction—a magnetic pull, so to speak—toward topics and ideas that seem unusual, excessive, or lacking in meaning to those around them.

This strong pull of attention often occurs at the cost of not engaging in things that others would consider more important for independent living such as making life goals, attending school, or taking the car in for service. The ASD individual feels his unique interests are very important, whereas these other independent behaviors seem to lack importance and are not compelling in any meaningful way. She feels no compulsion or motivation to achieve broader goals, and no amount of coaxing and reasoning from others can shift that difference in priorities.

An example of a highly fixated interest or an unusual attachment to objects may be seen when an ASD individual has a collection of 1200 aluminum can tabs that he sorts on a regular basis. Another individual spends seven hours a day making spreadsheets of temperature readings taken from the backyard, the front yard, and inside the home, and then he graphs trends over various periods of time. These individuals experience a strong "magnetic" attraction to these activities. These behaviors are not harmful in any way; rather, the intense involvement in these activities is out of proportion with the rest of the individual's life in terms of self-care, responsibilities, and commitments.

In contrast, the neurotypical individual typically would not find satisfaction collecting hundreds of pop can tabs. Similarly, although weather may be of interest to many, the neurotypical person would not feel that "magnetic" pull toward expending several hours a day gathering weather information around her home and graphing trends, with no eventual purpose for collecting this data other than to collect it. Some of the "magnetic" interests of the ASD individual may be somewhat understandable ("I like watching Cubs games too"), although the granular level of fixation differentiates the autistic's interest from the typical interest of others who enjoy a similar activity. For example, the autistic may prefer to watch only the baseball stats on his cell phone app during a game, whereas the neurotypical individual prefers to watch the game, is interested in certain players and the reactions of the crowd, and enjoys the good-natured fun of team rivalries during the game.

The frontal-subcortical systems of the brain are supposed to enable us to latch on to topics of interest and hobbies if they are meaningful and purposeful. Even though hobbies are pursued for enjoyment, they also have a relevant outcome: sewing produces a new dress; gardening produces a beautifully landscaped yard or vegetables to eat; one's study of archeology increases one's knowledge or adds to the body of knowledge available on that subject when your research is posted on your website or written in a book.

The daily weather tracking on spreadsheets would be relevant if the individual uploaded that information to websites that track local weather, for example. However, doing this just for the sake of keeping track, particularly when it comes to tracking the internal temperature of the house when a thermometer or thermostat already does this qualifies this hobby as a magnetic and repetitive behavior with no meaningful purpose.

Our brain should allow us to release things from our attention if they are unimportant or no longer relevant. The autistic brain has a tendency to be drawn toward interests and objects with an inappropriate level of intensity without the ability to release oneself from it. Just as a magnet is reliably drawn toward iron or nickel, and clings with such force to those metals that it's hard to pry the magnet from them, the autistic brain may be drawn toward and stick to thoughts, ideas, interests, and behaviors that are not meaningful, useful, or within a clear context.

Practice the Concepts Learned

Take some time to dive into the concepts behind the physics of behavior by looking at each category and reading the example provided. Consider real life or hypothetical examples of behavior for each concept, and list those under the appropriate category.

The Pull Toward a Behavioral Default

What behaviors may be examples of an autistic individual "defying gravity" by acting outside her usual behavioral patterns?

Example 1: The ASD individual suppresses the urge to pace or rock during a family gathering.

Example 2 (write your own):

_____

_____

_____

_____

_____

_____

Inertia: Difficulty Switching Behavioral Gears

What behaviors in the ASD individual may represent inertia and require outside assistance or prompting to alter?

Example 1: George is a twenty-three-year-old in the spectrum who seems content to spend hours sitting on his parents' porch watching the birds and squirrels in the yard. He requires prompting from his parents to switch behavioral gears and complete other important goals, such as daily self-care and interacting with others.

Example 2 (write your own):

_____

_____

_____

_____

Behavioral Pushback or Resistance to Change

List examples of behaviors in the spectrum that may represent pushback or resistance to change.

Example 1: Mr. Johnson is a middle-aged gentleman who has lived in the same home since childhood. His parents are deceased, and his sister lives with her family in a nearby town. The home is old and needs significant structural and cosmetic repairs, but Mr. Johnson repeatedly tells his sister he doesn't feel the "time is right" to proceed with "her plans" for the house. She feels resistance from him whenever she brings up the topic.

Example 2 (write your own):

_____

_____

_____

_____

Momentum: The Tendency Toward Behavioral Repetition

Repetition of behaviors is often seen in the spectrum. The behaviors may be healthy or unhealthy, which means the repetition can work for or against the individual. Provide some examples of behavioral momentum where the established behaviors are easier to continue than to stop.

Example 1: Rose writes in her journal every night before sleep. Although writing in a journal has been a fruitful and comforting part of her nightly routine, she is currently sick in the hospital and unable to write with any clarity. The presence of her behavioral momentum for writing causes stress when the behavior must be altered or paused. Although she understands the facts of her situation, her brain leans toward the repetitive behavior of writing, thus resulting in her distress at being unable to do this activity while hospitalized.

Example 2 (write your own):

_____

_____

_____

_____

_____

Acceleration: Gaining Behavioral Intensity

Some behaviors gain momentum through repetition over time and are easier to continue than to suppress. Others gain momentum and accelerate in intensity. Think of some examples and list them below.

Example 1: Jacob was encouraged by his first grade teacher to chew every bite of food fifty times. As a fifty-year-old, he still chews repetitively, and he is now up to sixty-six chews per bite of food.

Example 2 (write your own):

_____

_____

_____

_____

_____

_____

_____

_____

Magnetism: The Forces of Behavioral Attraction

Individuals in the spectrum are often drawn "magnetically" toward certain ideas, interests, or topics. List some examples below.

Example 1: Melissa is fascinated by small animal skeletons and bones. She collects small bones and feathers, and sorts them by size and color, although the pieces are not particularly unique. She is not studying animal sciences, nor does she put her interest to meaningful use, and she lacks attention to more important daily goals such as cleaning her room and completing homework.

Example 2 (write your own):

_____

_____

_____

_____

_____

_____

_____

Chapter 3

Begin at the Beginning

*N*ow that we have learned some basic concepts and terms, let's talk about behavioral goals and plans for change. Because ASD is a neurologic condition that impacts behavior and social connections, behavioral goals often need to be established to increase well-being. Let us be clear, not every autistic characteristic needs to be altered; some are great gifts and are used to significant benefit. For example, an ASD individual who has a very keen attention to visual detail can detect errors and safety concerns in the environment very quickly. However, some ASD characteristics create barriers to well-being whether in the areas of safety and health, independence, social connection, and the achievement of the individual's life goals. With that in mind, the journey toward well-being through behavioral change is the focus of this book.

One of the most common errors when establishing a step-by-step plan to achieve behavioral goals, whether within or outside of the autism spectrum, is to start at the wrong place and build in expectations at various steps in the process that the individual is unable to meet.

Instead, let's make sure we begin at the beginning. As detectives, we approach goal setting by first gathering information. What behaviors does the ASD individual display that hinder his or her daily life and productivity? What would improvement look like? What types of events or environments trigger the behavior, make the behavior worse, or make the behavior better? Every behavior contains clues about what is happening inside the individual that leads to a certain reaction.

Remember, behavior is a form of communication. To maintain a positive environment while the autistic individual works toward behavioral goals, we must take the approach that we are translating the "language" of his or her communication to better understand what is at the root of the behavior. This should be done with an open mind and without lapsing into the tendency to categorize behaviors as solely or even primarily representing issues of motivation or personal character.

This chapter provides five steps to help make the process of assessment and behavioral goal setting as seamless as possible with the least resistance on the part of the individual and with positive, attainable outcomes. Steps 1, 2, and 3 prepare the individual for success. Steps 4 and 5 involve the actual process of behavioral change.

Step 1: Assess the ASD Individual's Strengths and Challenges

What are the individual's strengths and challenges? On a typical day, what is the ASD individual capable of doing? Understanding the abilities of the individual will guide the process of setting attainable goals.

This step of determining what a person is capable of is tricky because there is always some level of estimation required. No blood test or diagnostic scan can provide a print-out with strengths and challenges neatly listed in two columns. We must take the careful, methodical approach of a detective.

Another challenge in the area of determining patterns of ability is that ability may change over time. For example, some parents will note that their child's interaction with peers seemed age appropriate during early childhood when play dates were the norm, but as the child grew into adolescence, he seemed to lag behind his peers in the area of social connection. As his peers became involved in complex social interactions—school clubs and sports, church youth groups, scouting, and other group-based activities—the ASD adolescent was unable to keep up with this complexity and either refused to participate or had meltdowns and other stress responses when attempting to.

Another example of changing abilities would include the aging adult who demonstrates some decline in ability over time. Perhaps she has had a stroke, or has dementia that leads to a specific area of weakness not present in her younger years.

Although there is some level of estimation involved in this type of assessment, the first step toward understanding someone's strengths and challenges may include some formal testing of cognitive (thinking) and communication skills. For example, one individual may be able to comprehend one or two spoken sentences, but finds it difficult to understand whole paragraphs spoken to him at once. He misses detail and feels stressed when trying to keep up with the information coming his way. Another may be very good at processing verbal information, but has trouble understanding picture instructions for assembling a bicycle or a piece of furniture, for example.

If a formal assessment of thinking and communication is not available, try to look for clues in everyday living. For example, the individual who keeps misplacing items may have difficulty with working memory (keeping things "in mind") or she may have a deficit in visual scanning and attention, meaning, she is unable to visually scan a crowded or changing environment to detect details. Another person who keeps asking "What time do we leave?" may lack a good internal sense of time (time management is an executive function ability) or may be demonstrating repetitive verbalizations, common in the spectrum.

Gathering observations from daily life regarding the underlying abilities of the individual, such as those cited above, will help you generate hypotheses about the best approach to take. Being aware of the pattern of an ASD individual's abilities is an important foundation for building a stable behavioral plan. This is true for goal setting within and outside the spectrum, although individuals in the spectrum tend to have more significant peaks and valleys in their skill sets—that is, significant ability in one cognitive or academic area with notable impairment in another domain. A solid individual assessment within the spectrum, therefore, is vital as we "begin at the beginning."

Step 2: Filling and Draining Activities

The second step in the process is to understand what types of events or activities are soothing, filling, and calming to the individual. In contrast, seek to understand the activities that drain the individual and increase his or her stress level.

This step is separate from step one but may overlap in some ways. For example, if an individual has a weakness in the area of spatial/visual learning, he or she will have challenges learning directions in a new workplace or city. The process of navigating that new environment will be a draining activity for the individual and will lead to a heightened stress response.

In addition to aligning with strengths and weaknesses, we can look to the individual's special interests and "go-to" activities. The ASD individual who spends significant time watching YouTube videos likely finds this a soothing activity. The individual who collects coins is likely to find sorting through his collection a filling and restful way to spend an afternoon.

Observations of the individual's regular avoidance patterns may also be a clue as to what is draining. For example, many in the spectrum find the emotions of others draining. An ASD wife, for example, may avoid talking about difficult topics with her husband because of the strong emotions involved in the conversation.

Interruptions of behavioral patterns will also likely be draining. For example, if an individual in the spectrum has a specific sequence for completing daily activities, anything that interferes with that sequence will probably cause the individual to feel stressed and drained.

Likewise, the removal of objects or activities that have a "magnetic pull" for the individual will be draining. The individual who spends hours on his computer playing online role-playing games is likely to be very stressed by the sudden removal of his computer.

The individual in the spectrum may also identify sensory inputs that feel draining such as loud noises or scratchy clothing. There are also likely to be many sensory experiences that the individual identifies as soothing such as deep pressure, proprioceptive inputs (pulling, pushing, or hanging inputs in the joints such as heavy work or yoga), or vestibular (movement) inputs such as swinging or rocking. Although the individual may be able to identify some filling and draining activities on her own, it has been my experience that the ASD individual may not show strong self-awareness and therefore may miss her own reactions in varying circumstances.

To make a complete and useful evaluation, it helps to have observational input from partnering detectives such as family, friends, teachers, and medical staff. This all-points approach creates the most detailed and meaningful assessment of what is filling and draining for the individual in most situations and environments at various times of day, as well as when the individual is rested and wake, exhausted and tired, or hungry.

Step 3: Big-Picture Assessment

Thirdly, look at the big picture of the individual's daily life. In steps 1 and 2, we looked at the individual's unique characteristics—strengths and challenges, likes and dislikes. In this step, we look at the individual's daily life and environment. In addition to understanding her overall abilities and preferences, it is important to know if she has recently been ill, experienced hormonal changes, suffered a loss, or struggled with insomnia. In contrast, her environment may have new supports or the addition of coping strategies that help her overall functioning.

This big-picture assessment helps us know whether there are things in the individual's life that make him more or less resilient than usual. To the extent that draining events and activities have occurred in his life, he is likely to show less overall resiliency; likewise, he is likely to take longer to recover from draining activities than from neutral or filling activities.

Alternatively, perhaps the environment has been very supportive to the individual lately. If he is a student, maybe he has recently begun receiving assistance from an aide at school. In this case, he may show more resilience than was typical when he had a less supportive environment. Therefore, the big-picture assessment helps us predict the ASD individual's needs and behaviors in his current environment.

Once we have completed steps 1 through 3, we should have a sense of how the individual typically responds to her environment. To summarize:

- **Step 1:** One of her strengths is being able to immerse herself in reading for several hours, but she is overwhelmed with changing visual environments.
- **Step 2:** Perhaps others notice that she is soothed by resting under heavy blankets and is "filled up" after long walks in nature, but is drained by attending loud class assemblies.
- **Step 3:** When considering her recent and current environment, it is noted that she has entered puberty, has recently received a therapy dog, and has a new teacher at school.

The foundation has been laid for a successful behavioral plan. The next steps involve creating and implementing the plan.

Step 4: Create Appropriate Behavioral Goals

This fourth step focuses on the goal of behavior change. We can safely assume that a desired behavioral goal will increase the well-being and connectedness of the ASD individual. However, the goal itself will carry a demand on the individual, and understanding the specifics of that demand is crucial.

For example, let's assume you are having a family Christmas gathering at your home, and it would be wonderful if your brother Michael (who is on the spectrum) could also attend. Your brother wants to come, but he also feels drawn toward staying at home in his own space. You both know that attending the gathering will be a challenging goal for him, but hope it can be rewarding as well.

First, make a list of what this behavioral goal will demand of him:

- Leave the quiet and predictability of his own home.
- Leave his preferred objects and activities: playing games on his computer, watching YouTube videos, and sorting his collections of rare vintage playing cards.
- Enter a house that smells different from his home. He is very sensitive to smells and can feel overwhelmed by food and pet smells.
- Engage in interactions with other people in a crowded living space.
- Follow what people are saying when they speak multiple sentences in conversation before pausing to let him respond.
- Think of answers to open-ended questions such as, "So, what's new with you these days?"
- Think of questions to ask others.
- Smell and eat foods he does not usually have in his daily routine.
- Stay calm, not talk to himself, not rock back and forth.

- Stay for an indeterminate period (uncertainty in his schedule is stressful to him).

- Tolerate people brushing against him as they walk by or giving him hugs in greeting.

- Wear something "nice" instead of his usual sweatpants and t-shirt.

- Skip his usual home routine that day. He has a specific routine that he does not like to break or alter, and going to the gathering will mean he cannot complete the full string of his daily activities.

- Understand jokes, sarcasm, and other social ways of talking that convey subtle layers of meaning.

- Deal with people at the gathering who become loud or boisterous when drinking.

Because you have completed steps 1 through 3 already, you have a better understanding of how the demands of the goal (in this case attending a social gathering) may impact your brother. In order to create a viable plan for success, you will need to identify what a good outcome will look like, and also identify whether a balance of draining and filling activities and stimuli can be achieved for Michael as he attempts to defy gravity by leaving his behavioral default of being home alone in his comfortable routine.

Identify What a Good Outcome Will Look Like

Although attending the holiday gathering with family is the overall goal, you will need to determine what a good outcome will look like. For example, will attending the gathering for five minutes feel like a good outcome? Will talking to five different relatives be the measure of a good outcome?

Taking into account Michael's abilities and the demands of the task, perhaps you talk with him in a comfortable setting about the upcoming

Christmas gathering, and together you determine that a good outcome would include eating Christmas dinner with the family and opening his present before leaving.

Balance Filling and Draining Activities and Stimuli

Working together, you and Michael make a list of ways to balance the filling and draining portions of the gathering:

- Michael will be offered a role so he feels more secure in this social setting. In this case, Michael says he would feel comfortable taking people's coats into the first-floor study.

- You will have his favorite foods at the party even though they are not traditional Christmas dishes (e.g., creamy peanut butter on rice cakes, bananas, and milk).

- Michael will sit next to you and your son at the dinner table because he feels most comfortable with the two of you.

- You will create a quiet and comfortable space in a second-floor guest room where he can leave the main gathering room and enjoy some time alone on the computer at intervals.

- You will let him know what his Christmas present is ahead of time so it is not a stressful surprise. He will have a choice when the time comes of opening his present with the group or when he is at home alone so he won't have to negotiate the oohs and ahs of onlookers during the present exchange.

Because the first three steps were completed in advance of making behavioral goals, the foundation was laid to allow for appropriate goal setting and a good amount of supports to balance the draining and filling aspects of a typically stressful setting. A good outcome was defined, and Michael felt secure and successful as he attempted to defy his behavioral gravity. Although the gathering was still stressful to Michael, he felt good about what he accomplished and was able to recuperate fairly quickly at home afterward. He even brought you a deck of playing cards for your Christmas present.

In the next section, you will have an opportunity to practice the concepts presented in this chapter.

Practice the Concepts Learned

In this section, you will practice beginning at the beginning. Remember, you are a detective, behavior is a form of communication as well as revelation, and strategy is key. The first three steps should be completed before behavioral goals and plans are made.

1. Identify the Strengths and Challenges of the Individual

Take a moment to consider the individual strengths and challenges of the individual in the spectrum. Feel free to use real-life examples, or to create a hypothetical scenario like the one we used above. Some examples are listed to get you started.

Strengths:

Reading

Drawing

List some strengths of the ASD individual in your life:

_____

_____

_____

_____

_____

_____

_____

_____

Challenges:

Sitting still while listening to information

Finding words to express his thoughts when he is upset

List some challenges of the ASD individual in your life:

_____

_____

_____

_____

_____

_____

_____

2. Filling and Draining Activities
Based on your observations, list the activities, events, objects, sensory inputs, and interactions that have made the individual feel filled and content, and those that have made him/her feel drained. A sample has been provided for you.

Filling:

Sorting through her collection of ballerina figurines

List the filling activities of the ASD individual in your life:

_____

_____

_____

_____

_____

_____

_____

Draining:

> Being in crowded environments such as a mall or a church gathering

List the draining activities of the ASD individual in your life:

_____

_____

_____

_____

_____

_____

_____

1. Big-Picture Assessment: The Individual's Environment and Recent Events

Now that you have shown awareness of the ASD individual's strengths and challenges, as well as activities that are filling versus draining, take a moment to consider the larger picture of health, emotional events, and changes in life circumstance that may increase or decrease the resilience of the individual in your care who is in the spectrum:

_____

_____

_____

_____

_____

_____

_____

2. Create a Behavioral Goal

Help the individual determine the goals she is working toward. Perhaps she identifies these herself, or her family and/or support people help her set realistic goals. An example has been provided to spark your thinking.

Behavioral Goal:
Eat dinner at the table with the family.

Describe a behavioral goal for the ASD individual in your life:

_____

_____

_____

_____

_____

_____

_____

_____

Break down the specific demands of that goal:
Sit in a chair without leaving the table for at least thirty minutes.

Eat whatever dinner foods are served.

What are the specific demands of achieving the behavioral goal for the ASD individual in your life?

_____

_____

_____

_____

_____

_____

_____

_____

3. Create a Behavioral Plan

When you create a behavioral plan, the goal must be achievable. If the demands of the goal are too great for the individual, make the goal smaller and less demanding. Figure out the most important part of the goal and remove the unimportant parts. Create a doable, realistic plan that will bring success and provide appropriate supports to the individual at this time.

What would a successful outcome look like?

Stay at the table for ten minutes before leaving.

What would a successful outcome look like for the ASD individual in your life?

_____

_____

_____

_____

How can the draining and filling aspects of the goal be balanced so that the individual successfully achieves the goal?

The individual is allowed to squeeze a stress ball at the table.

The individual is allowed to wear a baseball cap to decrease visual inputs.

What would a successful outcome look like for the ASD individual in your life?

_____

_____

_____

_____

Chapter 4

The Consequences of Consequences

So far, we have approached the topic of behavioral change by identifying neurologic roots to autistic behavioral patterns and determining how to balance appropriate demands to encourage successful outcomes.

Now, what about the topic of disobedience, manipulation, and controlling behaviors? How do we effectively guide the ASD individual who does not complete required goals?

We begin at the beginning, as always. Because we are detectives, we investigate these behaviors to figure out the underlying messages they communicate. We do not do this in anger or retribution, or with a punishment mindset, but by using the fact-finding mission we discussed earlier. We also learn to leave our personal narrative at the door.

What do I mean by our personal narrative? Let's take the example of Kari, a fourteen-year-old in the spectrum. One day after school, her mother found Kari sitting in a dark closet using an electronic device to look through pictures of lizards, one of her special interests. Her mother has a narrative in her own mind about Kari's behavior, what it means, and how it should be addressed. She believes that Kari stole her electronic device in defiance of the household rule that says Kari cannot have more than thirty minutes of screen time per day. In the context of Mom's narrative about defiance, Mom punishes Kari by taking away all access to electronic devices indefinitely. Kari melts down and has such a significant outburst that she breaks a door off its hinges. Mother interprets this as further evidence of Kari's emotional manipulation and defiance.

Now, let's back away from Mother's narrative for a moment. Let's be detectives and list the facts we know about Kari:

The Physics of Kari's Behavior

Kari is a young woman in the spectrum with a magnetic attraction to pictures of animals, most recently lizards and other reptiles. She collects pictures and information about these animals in the same way that others collect stamps or bottle caps. She defies gravity when she attends school because she would prefer to be alone and withdrawn from the many complex social and sensory inputs of the school environment and the bus ride. Her brain tends toward repetition and has a momentum for visual information and for information about animals.

Kari's individual strengths include her very high visual reasoning, her affiliation toward visual detail and pictures, and her artistic ability. She has fairly good rote memorization skills and uses these to gather information about animals. She is three grade levels behind in reading, and has significant difficulty getting through chapters in her schoolbooks regardless of the topic. She struggles to understand the nuances of social communication and feels confused about the motives of others. She often feels isolated and misunderstood.

Kari is soothed when she looks at animal pictures. She also loves swimming underwater along the lengths of the community pool. This activity is relaxing to her because it feels like a big, silent hug. She finds school draining and comes home exhausted and very close to melting down. She has a tendency toward being overwhelmed rather than under-whelmed in her environment, and she leans toward fight-or-flight responses when she feels stressed. She is perfectionistic and hates to make mistakes.

Regarding Kari's big picture, she is currently experiencing the normal biologic changes associated with puberty. Her emotions feel like a roller coaster much of the time. She has established a supportive relationship with her school counselor and principal, and the school's management of her individualized educational plan (IEP) has been helpful and consistent. Her parents have been divorced for seven years, and her weekends with Dad are difficult to manage in the context of his relationship with his fiancé and her children. Kari's sleep has been more disturbed than usual, and she typically only gets four hours of good sleep per night.

Kari is being asked to follow multiple school and household rules. Among them (and highlighted in this example) is that Mother allows thirty minutes of screen time per day. Additionally, she is frustrated that Kari spends time looking at animals instead of completing her homework, finishing household chores, and attending to hygiene appropriately. Mother's goal is that Kari will come home from school, eat a snack from the list of healthy snacks provided, and complete school and household activities in the hours before bedtime. Mother allows Kari to choose when the thirty minutes of screen time fit into this schedule.

Kari's mother makes a point of mentioning that Kari was compliant and kind prior to middle school, at which time she became increasingly defiant and manipulative. Kari's mother describes her daughter's behavior as defiant because of the following reasons:

- **Inconsistency:** Kari sometimes follows the rules and achieves the behavioral goals set by her mother, and other times she doesn't. Therefore, Kari's mother believes that "Kari can meet the standard when she wants to," but that she manipulates the rules when she "doesn't want to."

- **Avoidance:** Mother notes that Kari knows the rules but actively avoids difficult tasks such as homework and chores so that she can engage in pleasurable activities. Because this seems deliberate, her mother labels this as sneaky behavior. She is adamant that the avoidant aspect and secrecy of the behaviors points to deliberate planning and therefore manipulation on Kari's part to gain pleasure (similar to someone hiding in the closet to eat forbidden ice cream).

- **Emotional Manipulation:** Mother sees Kari's meltdown as an attempt at emotional manipulation. Kari's behavior feels so threatening that her mother thinks Kari is punishing her for setting rules, making Kari do chores and homework, and limiting her screen time. She feels that if she doesn't punish the meltdown, she will be giving implicit permission for Kari to manipulate her.

Mother emphasizes that the defiant and controlling aspects of the behavior are more concerning than the screen time. Mother wants to "stamp out" any attempts at defiance with consistent consequences for bad behavior before they take root.

Instead of following Mother's line of reasoning that Kari is being deliberately defiant and manipulative, let's consider an alternate narrative, a way of explaining Kari's behavior that takes into consideration who she is as an autistic teenager.

Kari is in the autism spectrum. She has always been a perfectionist who strives to please others. Because she is an adolescent now, and no longer a young child, her hormones are causing greater extremes in emotion. Coupled with this, her academic and social world have become much more complex. By the time Kari gets through the school day and the bus ride home, she is on the verge of losing emotional control.

Kari is so desperate to regroup, soothe herself, and become filled up again that she hides in an enclosed space such as a closet—a form of flight behavior—and seeks activities that are filling. For her, these are visual activities involving animals. She avoids other chores and tasks, not out of manipulation and the pleasure of "bucking the rules," but in an attempt to regain much-needed equilibrium. Because her mother can't be convinced to allow Kari more time with her special interests, Kari feels the need to grasp at the interest by doing something that is against household rules. Although we could say Kari is trying to control the situation, this grasping at control is an attempt to recover from a very overwhelming day and to find a place of centeredness and calm. The behavior itself is revelation of how much she feels she needs this activity in order to function.

In other words, when we take the detective approach to the situation of Kari sitting in the closet looking at animal pictures on an electronic device, we are able to say, "This behavior is revelation. It is telling me something important about Kari's internal state. She has had a really hard day and is trying to regroup." That is much more realistic and effective than saying, "You're breaking the rules because you like being defiant."

If we consider this alternate narrative, we can see how the tightening of the rule about screen time as punishment for her breaking of the rule is enough to increase the intensity of stress and to precipitate an outburst. Mom inadvertently pushed Kari past the point of consolation when she was on the verge of an outburst to begin with. She left Kari without a way of soothing herself and failed to see the desperation Kari felt when she hid in the closet.

Let's consider some of Mom's observations of Kari's behavior and address them as they pertain to individuals in the autism spectrum.

Inconsistent Behaviors

One of the most frequent comments I hear is, "Well, I've seen him do it (the expected good behavior), so I know he can when he wants to." The speaker is observing that the individual's follow through with "good behavior" is inconsistent. This inconsistency is taken as evidence of willfulness, of wanting or not wanting to achieve a certain behavioral goal.

Although ambivalence about a goal can cause anyone to approach it half-heartedly, resulting in inconsistent behavior depending on whether they feel like it at any particular time, inconsistency is also an indicator of a behavioral weakness. That is, the presence of inconsistency lets us know which behaviors are difficult for the individual to accomplish in a consistent and thorough manner. For example, I have a friend who runs marathons, but it would be unrealistic to expect her to run one every day if she "wanted to."

When working with an individual in the autism spectrum, keep in mind that the inconsistency of a particular behavior is a clue that the behavior is difficult, draining, or stressful for the individual, just as marathon running is difficult and draining, and puts stress on the body.

Avoidant Behaviors

Although an ASD individual's behavior may seem controlling because she resists difficult activities and prefers to spend most of her time doing pleasurable activities, this is not necessarily an indicator of bad intent. If we act as a detective and realize that the things she avoids are draining for her in her current environment, we can take stock of what is filling for her. We may see that the draining and filling aspects of her day are quite imbalanced. This compels us to want to help her learn how to balance the draining and filling parts of her day. This is what she is attempting to do when she hides in the closet to look at animal pictures. In this case, her avoidance of certain activities is revelation to an onlooker of what is draining for her. Her secretive way of grasping at pleasurable activities also gives us information about how she copes with feeling overwhelmed, and it reflects her attempts to get her needs met while avoiding her mother's displeasure and recrimination.

Emotional Manipulation

We typically see emotional meltdowns and outbursts in younger children. These meltdowns may reflect exhaustion, not feeling well, or an intentional display of displeasure to get something they desire (e.g., I will kick and scream until you give me another cookie).

Although emotional meltdowns are not as expected for fourteen-year-olds as they are for toddlers, we do know that a core difficulty among individuals in the autism spectrum is the ability to regulate emotions: staying calm in intense situations; expressing certain emotions and leaving other emotions unexpressed; choosing when, where, and how to express emotions. Rather than viewing Kari's emotional outburst as akin to kicking and screaming until she gets another cookie, it is more realistic to see it as a sign of being overwhelmed.

Let's keep in mind the trio of behaviors—fight, flight, and freeze—seen in ASD individuals who are overwhelmed by their environments. Kari showed flight (hiding in the closet) and fight (melting down and damaging the door) as a consequence of being overwhelmed at the end of her day and not being allowed as much time to look at animal pictures online as she wanted. The underlying reason for *why* she wanted to look at animal pictures in the closet was because she innately knew that she *needed* to engage in that activity to feel centered and calm. In other words, she needed to refill her very drained battery.

If we see her meltdown as a clue to her stress level and inability to self-regulate rather than as a tool of manipulation, we can approach goal setting in a more appropriate and successful manner.

If we let go of the assumption that Kari's behavior is conniving, we can view the episode as revelation that her emotional scales have tipped, and she has become dysregulated in the midst of an overwhelming environment. The draining parts of her environment have overcome the filling parts, and she feels rattled, overwhelmed, and undone.

The Problem with Punishment

A reliance on consequence or punishment to improve behavior is usually unsuccessful because it involves the following assumptions. For individuals in the autism spectrum, these assumptions are often incorrect:

- **Assumption #1:** The individual receiving the consequence is capable of accomplishing the demand or request but chooses not to.

- **Assumption #2:** Even though the individual is able to regulate his emotions and the resulting behaviors, he has frequent emotional outbursts due to spite or willfulness.

- **Assumption #3:** The individual has access to tools, strategies, and supports to help her regulate her behavior and achieve desired outcomes, such as meeting daily goals, but she stubbornly refuses to use those.

Unfortunately, in the example of Kari, her attempts to escape an overwhelming environment and engage in a favorite activity have usually led to punishment from her mother. Being denied access to her favorite activity creates strong emotions in Kari that are more difficult to regulate than the stress she already feels from a long day at school. When her mother takes away this activity, Kari is being asked to achieve a behavioral goal that she literally cannot achieve. In her dysregulated state, it is nearly impossible for her to follow the rules and maintain appropriate calm with her mother, which leads to her emotional outburst and meltdown.

Her mother's punishment leads to worse outcomes because it does not recognize the root of Kari's behavior: the heightened level of dysregulation that compelled her to go into the closet in the first place, and the negative impact of taking away the soothing activity of looking at animal pictures.

Although some behavioral professionals might encourage the mother to use consistent and unyielding consequences for Kari's "bad" behavior, this approach is bound to fail a good deal of the time because Kari is an individual in the autism spectrum. Unless her mother, her teachers, and other caregivers in her life understand the physics of her behavior, begin at the beginning, approach the situation like a detective, and use strategies to improve her behavioral regulation, Kari and her mother will continual to spiral in a never-ending vicious cycle that leaves both feeling frustrated, angry, and lost.

It is also important to understand the difference between punishment—in this case taking away possessions that bring entertainment—and logical consequences. The problem with punishment is that it often involves shame and the exertion of control from the caregiver to force behavioral change through an uncomfortable outcome.

Logical Consequences

In contrast, a logical consequence is an outcome that is directly linked to the behavior. As its name implies, it is the logical consequence of an action. No shame is involved with this method because it links the consequence to the action/behavior and not to the individual. For example, not having money to buy a video game because you spent your money on candy is a logical consequence of how you chose to spend your money. Having ants in your room may be the logical consequence of leaving food sitting out instead of throwing it in the garbage.

One might ask whether logical consequences are always appropriate for the ASD individual when seeking behavioral change. After all, a logical response is less painful, less likely to be given in frustration, and not based on shame or fear. However, we must first remember our commitment to begin at the beginning, and consider what the person is capable of doing. For example, some ASD individuals show very significant and core symptoms of impulsivity, and are incapable of effectively thinking ahead and planning their budget in a logical way to avoid financial difficulties. Similarly, the ASD individual with a messy room may lack the behavioral initiation and sequencing needed to independently accomplish room cleaning thoroughly and on a consistent basis. Again, we must base everything on what the person is capable of doing before we determine what we can expect from him/her and what an appropriate response might be to the behaviors displayed.

We should also look at how serious or negatively impactful the logical consequence would be. It may be that we have determined that teaching the ASD individual about basic money skills is appropriate within the context of supervised learning over time. Perhaps a caregiver or family member meets with him daily to look at the calendar and talk through his options for when to pay specific bills and how to manage his money after he meets those obligations. In that instance, it may be determined that having to wait to purchase a video game because of lack of funds is an appropriate logical consequence to spending his money on candy.

However, caregivers must keep in mind that having a "logical consequence" of losing his apartment because he was allowed to spend his rent money on potato chips would be so negative as to be out of proportion for the skill being taught at the expense of the health and safety of the individual. The logical consequence, if anticipated as part of the learning process, should not be unsafe or potentially debilitating to the individual. Furthermore, large-scale consequences such as being evicted from his apartment can be avoided with the careful daily management, overseen by a skilled caretaker, of spending habits, cleanliness, management of noise levels, and other factors that if ignored could bring about eviction.

When creating appropriate goals for the ASD individual, it is important that there be some challenge in order to promote growth but also have the goal set up for success. One rule of thumb is to create goals in which the individual can complete at least 75 percent of the goal independently, with the need for only 25 percent (or less) assistance.

That is, the person may need help to navigate and complete a task, but this may only involve check-ins, redirection, or bits of advice on what to do next. Making sure a successful outcome is possible and appropriate supports are in place is critical to ensure that the individual experiences some challenges and encounters new learning, but is not overwhelmed by demands that she is incapable of meeting.

Additionally, as described in the book *Smart but Scattered* by Dawson and Guare (2011), the individual should not have to exert effort greater than a 3 on a 1 to 10 scale where 10 is the most effort possible, such as planning a wedding or packing your house to move. Having level 3 as a goal ensures that the overall effort of the day, week, and month is realistic and sustainable rather than overwhelming. That is, the individual is being asked to complete multiple tasks over a period of time, not just one task during a particular day. We can do level 10 tasks infrequently and with large gaps of time between them, but level 3 tasks are ones we can perform regularly and with consistency. If the task requires more effort than a level 3, consider changing the task to decrease the demand.

The following are some general guidelines to help the ASD individual experience logical consequences that he or she is able to respond to:

- **Make the task smaller.** Instead of giving the vague and generic instruction to "clean your room," ask her to put her books on the bookshelf. After a break during which she has spent time on an activity she enjoys, she may be asked to put her dirty clothes in the laundry hamper. Each piece of the request may require a level 3 effort, whereas the whole task would have been in the level 7 to 8 range, and thus overwhelming.

- **Give structure to the task.** Instead of giving the generic instruction to "get ready for bed," make the request more specific. Provide a checklist with words or pictures that convey what getting ready for bed means: take a shower, put on your pajamas, and brush your teeth.

- **Teach strategies to help the individual succeed.** If the individual is unable to have regular success with a task, help her find a better approach. For example, if the individual regularly melts down when interrupted, try saying, "I understand that you do not like being interrupted, but it seems like melting down just makes us both feel worse. What if I come in and set your visual timer to five minutes, and then I'll leave your room and shut the door behind me. That way, you'll have five minutes to prepare for the interruption that will be coming, and you won't feel surprised when I knock on your door. Should we try that, or do you have another idea about how to make things better?" This approach shows the individual that you want her to succeed with the behavior change, and you are willing and able to partner with her toward better outcomes.

- **Whenever possible, use rewards as incentives rather than punishments as the result of consequences.** I'm not advocating that there is never a reason for using consequences to achieve behavior change. I do know, however, from experience working with many individuals in the spectrum that other strategies are often more successful in the long term. The use of rewards can be very satisfying for the individual. The good news is that ASD individuals often have strong special interests or preferred sensory experiences that can be motivating for them. For example, instead of taking away a preferred activity as punishment for not completing chores, you could use the above suggestions to help with chore success and then offer access to the preferred activity as a well-earned reward. For example, you may let the individual know that she can earn thirty minutes of her preferred activity for every chore completed, up to a total of three hours per day. This gives the individual control over her achievement, which can help her attain balance between chore completion and pleasurable activities.

- **Stay calm and respectful at all times.** I know this can be difficult, but heightened emotion from a caregiver can quickly escalate the emotions of the ASD individual. For the autistic individual who has difficulty staying calm and focused, dealing with emotional escalation and pressure from a caregiver can quickly intensify a problematic situation, creating more pushback and resistance from the individual. Instead, try acknowledging and labeling his strong reactions to help him recognize them: "I understand that you feel so frustrated right now because I walked into your room without knocking first," or "I know that reading about dogs is very important to you." Next, be respectful of his preferences and difficulties by letting him know that you understand: "You are important to me," or, "I want you to have things in your day that you enjoy," or, "I don't want you to feel overwhelmed in this situation. What can we do to make things better?" For the ASD individual who may have trouble using words to describe what he is feeling, and who experiences difficulty calming down, this type of interaction can feel stabilizing, and therefore will lead to better outcomes for all involved.

- **Do not use consequences or punishments that take away the individual's ability to soothe, comfort, and self-regulate.** For example, one individual may regulate herself by spinning in her chair. If you are asking her not to spin at work because it is disruptive and unsafe for others, what will you offer her to replace this strategy? If another individual finds watching YouTube anime videos soothing when he feels overwhelmed, what will you offer him for self-soothing if you take away the videos? Keep this Catch-22 in mind when responding to problematic behaviors. Instead of taking away a self-regulation strategy, you may respond by saying, "I can see that you are using a strategy to feel better. Good job. Strategies are so important, but spinning in your chair is distracting to your coworkers. What if we have you sit on an exercise ball and move around on that while working? How does that feel? Maybe you could take five-minute spinning breaks in a separate, quiet room every hour. Would that help?" Rather than merely telling her to stop spinning, you are offering the individual alternative strategies for behavior regulation.

In this chapter, we have discussed some possible pitfalls of relying solely or primarily on punishment and consequences to manage or control the behavioral challenges of the autistic individual. Remember, be realistic in your expectations, acknowledge the desires and existing strategies of the individual, and be part of the solution. Resist responding in a way that escalates negative reactions and leaves the individual without the core calming strategies s/he needs to thrive.

How might Kari's story have had a different outcome? Consider this scenario:

Kari's mother notices that Kari is not doing her homework, but instead is hiding in the closet. Kari has taken Mother's electronic device and is looking at lizard pictures. Mother feels frustrated but reminds herself, *This tells me that Kari is feeling drained today*. Mother says, "It looks like you had a stressful day. Does being in the closet feel good? And I see you are looking at lizards. I know they are your favorite."

Perhaps Mother gives Kari a little more alone time in the closet before returning to talk to her again. When she does, she asks if there is a way Kari can feel better while also completing her household chores and homework, and following the guidelines for behavior that the family has agreed on.

After much trial and error, Kari and her mother devised the following plan with the help of her teachers and school administrators:

1. Although Kari's school was very supportive, it was determined that her school day was so significantly draining that it was causing quick triggers toward emotional dysregulation at home. To adjust her schedule, the school took Kari out of a few of her honors classes and placed her into regular coursework. They also allowed her to take two of her classes online at home, which shortened her school day by one and a half hours. Her mother picked her up from school so she wouldn't have to ride the noisy, crowded school bus at the end of the day.

2. Kari's mother realized that looking at reptile pictures was very important and soothing to Kari. She also wanted to find ways to repair their strained relationship. She and Kari decided to set aside thirty minutes a day when they would both sit down to look at reptile books from the library. Kari would show her mother the pictures she liked and tell her some interesting facts about each reptile. This achieved the reduction in screen time her mother was hoping for, and it helped them do a preferred activity together, which strengthened their bond. It also created a predictable time and place for Kari to enjoy her favorite soothing and filling activity.

3. Mother kept a list of items that Kari would like to buy. These had to do with her special interest in reptiles and her sensory preferences for fruity lotions and fidget spinners. Mother assigned the items certain point values, and she assigned point values to household tasks and homework completion. When Kari had completed her chores and assignments, she could buy an equivalent item from her preference list with the points she had earned. This helped her accomplish difficult tasks as she worked toward a preferred goal.

4. Mother and Kari realized that certain sensory activities were calming to Kari. They capitalized on her love of being underwater by going to the community pool four times a week. Kari wore earplugs to cut down on the sounds at the pool, and she primarily swam underwater for the deep-pressure feeling her body needed. In addition, as a family Christmas present, Kari's parents invested in a Jacuzzi that fit perfectly under their second-floor deck. The water was deep enough to feel relaxing and had massaging jets. It was private under the deck and without noise or distractions. Kari utilized this strategy after school to attain internal equilibrium and a sense of calm.

5. Kari had not been sleeping well, and this interfered with her emotional resilience during the day. Kari and her mom conferred with her primary care physician who suggested the natural supplement Melatonin for sleep support. After a bit of trial and error to find the correct dose, Kari was able to achieve about six and a half hours of sleep each night, which helped support her emotional regulation throughout the day.

Before implementing these strategies, Kari was uncomfortable in most aspects of her daily life, and she was unable to stabilize herself. She had a strained relationship with her mom, and they both felt unhappy about that and wanted it to improve. By using detective work and implementing an effective behavioral plan, Kari experienced successful daily outcomes.

Practice the Concepts Learned

1. Leave your narrative at the door

Sometimes we approach a situation with a narrative already in place— a particular mindset, an explanation of why certain things happen and what motives other people might have.

Can you think of a time when your narrative got in the way of accurately assessing, perceiving, or understanding a certain situation?

Write an example from your own life or a hypothetical example that demonstrates this concept.

_____

_____

_____

_____

2. Inconsistency and Motivation
Provide examples of when inconsistent behavior may reflect a lack of motivation.

_____

_____

_____

_____

Provide examples of when inconsistent behavior reflects a struggle to accomplish a goal consistently, thus revealing an area of behavioral weakness.

_____

_____

_____

_____

3. Avoidant and Controlling Behaviors
There are times when an ASD individual will attempt to control his environment to decrease anxiety. Write some examples of what this might look like in his or her daily life.

_____

_____

_____

_____

_____

4. Emotional Outbursts

What might an emotional outburst or meltdown signify in an individual within the spectrum? How might your reaction intensify or calm the reaction of the individual?

_____

_____

_____

_____

_____

5. Challenging Behavioral Goals

Some behavioral goals are listed below. As you think about each one, brainstorm some ways to make the goals appropriate in difficulty for an individual in the autism spectrum. Some examples are provided. On the blank lines, describe some ways each goal can be accomplished successfully by the ASD individual in your life.

Behavioral Goal: "You need to save more money."

This goal could be more specific and structured with clearly defined and attainable goals. For example, one initial goal may be to put ten dollars in savings after essential bills are paid and before money is spent on other interests.

How might the challenging goal of saving money be accomplished by the ASD individual in your life?

_____

_____

_____

_____

_____

_____

_____

Behavioral Goal: "Please be nice when family comes to visit."

The goal should be more specific. The individual could be told to use a softer tone of voice when upset. She could be asked not to swear when speaking to others. The individual will likely need concrete behavioral examples of what to do rather than the more conceptual "be nice."

How might the behavioral goal of being nice be accomplished by the ASD individual in your life?

_____

_____

_____

_____

_____

Behavioral Goal: "Watch your sister while I answer the door."

_____

_____

_____

_____

_____

Behavioral Goal: "Take charge of putting together the annual report for our director while I work on the product reviews."

_____

_____

_____

_____

_____

Behavioral Goal: "Start packing for the move. We only have four weeks before the new owners move in."

_____

_____

_____

_____

_____

_____

_____

Chapter 5

Self-Monitoring and Planning

*A*n important part of behaving appropriately in any situation is being able to monitor how we feel, whether physically or emotionally.

- Am I tired?
- Am I anxious?
- Am I sick?
- Am I frustrated?
- Am I cold?
- Am I sad?

Ideally, we are able to discern what causes us to feel the way we do, what clues there are that this state is emerging, how strong the state is, and what we can do to alter the state. An individual has self-monitored when she is able to say, *I'm tired and worried because I stayed up late last night with my sick child. I have a difficult meeting at work after lunch. I'm likely to be less able to stay calm than usual. I will plan to take a walk in the park during my lunch break to get centered before the meeting. That should help.*

The autistic individual is less able to monitor his or her internal state, whether physical or emotional, as compared to the neurotypical individual. An appropriate goal is to teach the ASD individual some self-monitoring skills. Although the individual may continue to have difficulty in this area, any progress toward better monitoring will likely improve outcomes.

Tools for Monitoring Internal States

Depending on the intellectual level of the ASD individual, a strategy can be as simple as assigning a color to his overall state. For example, you may choose red to represent red-hot anger and blue to represent blue-water calm. At various times throughout the day, you may ask him what "color he is feeling."

Another indicator tool can be an arrow that points to the left, right, or anywhere in between an arc (like a gas or pressure gauge) to represent an internal state.

A third tool uses a number scale from 1 to 10 to register levels, with 1 representing a very low presence of an internal sensation, and 10 being the very strong levels of the sensation. The individual may keep a written record of his internal state using this number scale, or he may use another strategy like putting a magnetic number on the fridge so that others can see his state as well. This method of self-monitoring and communicating internal states takes away any pressure the autistic individual might feel about speaking face to face with someone while also allowing others to know how he or she is doing.

Aside from the type of indicator chosen—colors, arrows, numbers, or whatever works best—the internal state being monitored can vary according to the needs of the individual. For one person, monitoring anger may be a good goal. For another person, monitoring stress or pain or fatigue may be more important. Choose which state, whether physical or emotional, is most meaningful for the individual at that time.

Noticing Trends

Looking for trends, determining cause and effect, and assessing the impact of coping strategies on the individual's emotional states may be something that a helper is primarily responsible for, but some ASD individuals can perform this type of self-assessment independently. The goal of the self-monitoring exercise is for the individual to become familiar with his or her typical internal state—stressed, energetic, anxious, or fatigued, for example—and to recognize what causes variations from that. This understanding will make it easier to implement an appropriate coping strategy to help the individual achieve a more regulated internal state on a more frequent basis.

Consider the following scenario:

Sandy is a forty-seven-year-old professional photographer whose fifty-six-year-old brother George is now living in her home. George was diagnosed with autism spectrum disorder at age twelve and is no longer able to work. While Sandy is at work, George is successful at being independent at home, but he vacillates between feeling sluggish and unmotivated to getting worked up and agitated throughout the day at the slightest provocation.

Sandy and George agree that he will use a 1 to 10 scale where 1 represents sleepy, foggy, or sluggish, 5 means that he feels just right, and 10 means that he feels restless, upset, and hyper. To Sandy's surprise, George asks her to use the same scale to measure her own states so they can share information about their day. Sandy agrees so that George will feel supported in this endeavor. They decide that whenever George is at home, he will write his numbers on a white board every hour using an alarm on his phone to remind him, and Sandy will keep a list of her own numbers in her work notebook.

George connected with this exercise because he has always liked numbers, and he appreciates having something to keep track of throughout the day. This hourly checking-in is new to him but feels rhythmic and predictable. It gives him some sense of what is coming next during his daily schedule. Sandy is also surprised at how helpful she finds the process for herself. She realizes that she often works through her day without much conscious awareness of how her physical, mental, and emotional energy levels change and why.

After a month of this new tradition, Sandy and George realize that his energy level tends toward sluggishness for several hours in the morning and doesn't pick up until around noon. In the afternoon, he becomes more active around the house, but quickly turns to irritation and over-reactive behaviors. For example, he likes to watch the national news network, but his strong opinions on geopolitical events often lead to shouting matches with the television. Although he enjoys a good debate about hot button topics, the passion he feels quickly changes to agitation, and it is very difficult for him to calm down afterward. George discovers that he feels calm and alert from around 11:00 p.m. to 2:00 a.m. During these three hours, he does not feel as quickly pulled to sluggishness or to agitation.

Another benefit of using this tracking system was that Sandy and George had a way of sharing with each other about their internal states. Sandy better understood what George was feeling and when. George could see by looking at Sandy's numbers at the end of the day that other people fluctuate in their internal states too. Sometimes he looked at her numbers and asked questions such as, "Why were you an 8 here?" He became more aware that other people's internal states move up and down in ways that do not mirror his own.

The next step in the journey was to figure out what triggered their internal states. Sandy noticed that she came out of a sluggish morning state by taking a hot shower, doing ten minutes of yoga, and eating a breakfast with a good balance of protein and complex carbohydrates. She kept her focus at work by setting her alarm to walk for five minutes or to climb up and down two flights of stairs every hour. She calmed down from stressed and upset states by listening to music, rolling her foot over a lacrosse ball, or walking in the park. Once home from work, she shrugged off the workday and entered into a calmer and more relaxed state by running a mile before taking a lavender bubble bath.

Sandy and George worked together to understand his states and their fluctuations. This was a bit more difficult for George to figure out and put into words, but they communicated openly with each other and were able to identify what led to improvement and what did not. His sluggish early to mid-morning state was consistent regardless of how much sleep he'd had the night before.

The only thing that seemed to break George out of this state was some type of proprioceptive input or vestibular input. (See chapter 5 of *Understanding Autism in Adults and Aging Adults 2nd Edition* for sensory strategies to impact internal states.) To achieve these, he started a routine of doing two one-minute planks and walking around the block after breakfast. Although he enjoyed following national events and politics, he didn't like feeling so worked up that he paced and shouted around the house for hours. Sandy and George were able to figure out that staying up to date on political events by reading articles on the internet was less likely to send George up to higher numbers on the stress scale than watching a TV program with individuals talking in escalated voices heightened with emotion as they debated the issues. Some programs agitated George more than others, so he decided to only watch the program that did not get him worked up. He eventually discovered that when he did reach an escalated state, lying prone under a weighted blanket and drinking hot tea with honey restored him to a sense of calm.

Sandy and George were not always successful in altering sluggish or heightened internal states when they wanted to, but their regulation was improved overall, as was their communication with each other, and they felt they had accomplished many good things in the process.

Improvements in self-monitoring can decrease the frequency of fight, flight, and freeze responses in the ASD individual, increase alertness and concentration when s/he feels sluggish, and promote open communication with others without having to use words laden with emotion.

Practice the Concepts Learned

Think about the ASD individual in your life who you would like to guide in the process toward effective self-monitoring. What type of tool might work best with his or her personality, interests, strengths, and preferences? Does he prefer music and art as a way to express how he feels? Is she fascinated with statistics, charts, and numbers, and is motivated to track her internal states by charting a graph? Does he love superheroes and villains, preferring to use one character to express that he feels angry and another character to express that he feels happy?

Brainstorm some thoughts and ideas below:

_____

_____

_____

_____

After careful thought and open communication to explore the individual's interests, use these ideas to develop a self-monitoring strategy that can be implemented most easily into daily life. No matter what strategy the individual uses in a certain season of life, teaching the ability to better understand internal states is something that can be used to improve many aspects of life.

Chapter 6

Adding Definition and Decreasing Intensity in Daily Life

One of the barriers to appropriate engagement for the ASD individual, whether social interaction, household tasks, or setting goals, is the vast and undefined world that must be managed. The lack of specific definition in life increases with adulthood. The emerging adult is expected to determine her life path, connect with others in increasingly complex ways, and manage conflict and difficulty in an appropriate manner.

As adulthood emerges, previous life experiences that were specific and definitive are now undefined. For example, a fourth grader attends school on a set schedule and completes homework assigned to him by the teacher, whereas an adult must choose what she wants to study in college or where he wants to work. Although intuitively we may think that freedom and multiple choices are a good thing, an individual in the spectrum may feel anxiety, confusion, and/or analysis paralysis—overanalyzing the options to the point of paralysis in decision making and action.

In the case of the ASD individual who feels paralyzed in his environment and unsure of how to move forward, specific strategies may be of assistance.

Offer Specifics when Communicating

The autistic individual is likely to have difficulty inferring someone's meaning and translating communications into specifics. An example is when Mom says, "Find something useful to do!" A neurotypical individual may understand without needing further explanation that Mom is stressed about relatives coming to visit in a few hours and needs help cleaning the house.

If you would like better interactions with an individual in the spectrum, try communicating with specifics rather than concepts. Rather than saying, "I want you to care more about my interests," the speaker may try saying, "Finishing my degree is really important to me. When I shared with you that I may not graduate this semester, I wanted you to ask me how I was feeling and what I needed." An ASD adolescent recently told me, "I just learned that when someone is crying and says 'leave me alone' they actually mean 'I want you to ask me what is the matter.'" This "translation" of communication into actual meaning was a learning process for the adolescent that she was able to use to adjust her behavior in the future.

The same concept is true when you ask the individual to complete tasks. "Clean up around here while I am at work," or "Try to think of ideas for Joey's birthday party" are likely too conceptual and without enough specific direction to be useful. The lack of structure can feel overwhelming.

With the autistic individual, the adage "It goes without saying" is often not true. Providing details and specifics is one way of adding structure to a situation that otherwise would feel amorphous and vague.

Offer Specific Choices

The autistic may experience the world as vast and undefined in a way that feels uncomfortable or confusing. When we say to someone, "It's up to you—do what you want," we are offering her more vastness than she can conceptualize, and providing no additional structure or definition. If you offer specific choices, you are providing structure, predictability, and definition. What was vast and undefined is now more understandable and manageable.

Consider the following examples:

- Mark is told by his 9th grade teacher that he should write an essay on anything related to WWII.
- Kassandra is asked what she wants for dinner on her birthday. Her mother says she can request any meal or choose any restaurant.
- After high school graduation, Suzi is told she should figure out whether she wants to get a job or go to college, what job or college she may wish to attend, and what she wants her major to be. It is her choice. It is up to her.

In reality, Mark, Kassandra, and Suzi would have felt more calm and energized by some type of structure or specifics in these requests. When they are given vague, general instructions, they are deluged with internal questions: Where to start? How to narrow down choices? Perhaps a helper could say to Mark, "Would you like to write about a person or a battle?" This offer builds structure into the assignment and provides definition to the paralyzing vastness of such a broad topic.

Offer Additional Time and Space

Rather than trying to reason with an ASD individual when he is overwhelmed—"What happened? Why are you feeling this way?" or, "Why are you so upset? It's not the end of the world!"—focus on calming strategies, and wait to analyze the reaction until he is in a calmer state. This waiting period is a way of building emotional space between him and the intense moment he was experiencing. A better way to communicate in this situation would be, "I see that this is overwhelming for you. Let's wait until there is more space and time between you and this situation. Then we can figure out what happened."

Of course, we all know that time is not always available. Sometimes an emergency must be dealt with immediately. Likewise, even when given emotional space, some ASD individuals will put off processing the hard topics indefinitely. But for many autistics, having more time to transition to a calmer state can bring about better results.

A caregiver can also offer physical space while talking to the ASD individual about difficult topics. If talking face to face is overwhelming, offer the option of emailing or texting. Perhaps the person could write a letter or note to you and leave it on your desk. Maybe you could sit back to back while speaking instead of face to face. Offering space is a gift for the individual who experiences the world as too intense. It's a way of saying, "Let me help you turn down the intensity."

Utilize Rehearsal and Social Stories

One way to build structure and predictability into an ambiguous or new situation is to create a social story or to physically or mentally rehearse the situation. Please see Chapter 9 of my book *Understanding Autism in Adults and Aging Adults 2nd Edition* for a full discussion of social stories and rehearsal. Rehearsing a situation may include physically walking through the situation ahead of time; driving someplace new a few days before you need to be there to make sure you can find the location and you know how long it takes to get there; looking up photos online of a new doctor or a person with whom you will be interviewing for a position. Rehearsal may also include mental imaging and rehearsing. In the case of a social story, the individual may tell themselves the story of what will happen at the appointment, meeting, family gathering, and so on. The social story for the adult can even be turned into a type of meditation tool to visualize and rehearse the story before an upcoming event.

The following is an example of a social story:

Before the first day of college, Maggie searches online for photos of the buildings on campus that will be part of her class schedule and dorm life. She compiles the photos in a book that tells the story of her first day. Then she tells herself that story: "Maggie has waited for this day a long time. She feels excited and nervous. She is worried she won't be able to find her classes, but then she remembers that she mapped out her whole schedule ahead of time. She wakes at six o'clock in the morning because she is forever the early bird. She walks six minutes to the campus cafeteria to eat eggs and bacon for breakfast. The warm food makes her feel stronger, and a hot tea is easy to take with her on the twelve-minute walk to her English Composition class on the second floor of Miller Hall (and so on…)."

Maggie tells herself this story and looks at the pictures many times before the actual first day of class. At the end of the story, she recites, "And this is how the first day of class goes unless something unexpected happens. Unexpected things happen every day, and that is okay." She leaves a blank page at the end of the story, and she plans to write down the unexpected things that happened at school. She knows she will probably fill in several things, but she doesn't know what they will be.

Keep a Record of Unexpected Occurrences

Another way of providing predictability and structure is to talk about how the unexpected is actually expected. The individual might find it helpful to write about the unexpected things that happen each day. In a household with other family members, it might be a tradition for each person to share his or her unexpected events with the family at dinnertime or during the evening before bed.

By creating a routine around unexpected events, we are making the unexpected expected. The unexpected is not without structure or a place of its own; indeed, it goes in its own special slot, which provides definition for the individual with ASD and can therefore decrease the stress of an unpredictable environment.

Make a Schedule

Sometimes life provides us with a schedule. In school or work environments, we may be handed certain times, places, and assignments to follow. However, during retirement or seasons of life in which that structure is not provided, the ASD individual can feel lost and without direction for daily activities. This can be seen in the autistic individual who sits around doing nothing, putters about the house aimlessly, or focuses only on special interests during his or her free time, leaving necessary daily life tasks undone.

One strategy to help the individual experience meaningful daily activities is to develop a schedule. This builds predictability and structure into his routine. He may decide to volunteer at the hospital every Monday from 10:00 a.m. to 2:00 p.m. He may take a walk through the park every Tuesday, Thursday, and Saturday morning from 7:00 a.m. to 8:00 a.m. You can see how the development of a schedule provides structure to the individual who otherwise might stall during an undefined day and be unable to complete healthy and meaningful activities without direction.

Create Rules and Guidelines

There are times when an ASD individual does not naturally transition into more mature roles as a neurotypical individual might do. As a way of making these transitions more specific and concrete, family members or helpers may wish to create rules and guidelines for transitions. Perhaps a twelve-year-old girl wants to hold her friend's hand when they walk together as a sign of affectionate friendship. She may need guidance to help her understand that preteens don't typically hold hands as they might have done with childhood friends. Mom could say, "You know what? You just turned twelve. This is a brand new year. You're in middle school now! Some things will be the same this year, and some things will be different. For example, twelve-year-olds don't hold hands with their friends. Sometimes, when people are just friends, they greet each other with a fist bump, a high five, or a greeting such as, 'Hey, how's it going?'.'"

This creation of rules can be helpful in many ways, but sometimes the rules can backfire as well. For example, the ASD individual may correct her peers if they are not "following the rules" as explained to her in her own home. Each situation is different, but guidelines and rules can help the ASD individual know how and when to transition to different behaviors.

How Big Is this Problem?

Create a rating scale as a way to build structure and guidelines around emotional reactions. The rating scale will differ depending on the age and situation of the ASD individual.

Let's consider the example of fifty-eight-year-old Phyllis who was diagnosed with an autism spectrum condition at the age of fifteen. She is currently working as a clerk in a clothing store, and has difficulty managing her anxiety when there is any kind of change in her work environment or schedule, when she makes mistakes, or when she has to deal with the heightened emotions of customers and colleagues. Her counselor helps her create a rating scale with some clues as to how she can evaluate the severity of the problems she encounters. The following is an example of this rating scale.

Level 1: Hiccup

Phyllis wanted to name a Level 1 problem a "hiccup." A hiccup includes an unexpected event that is small, can be fixed without assistance, and does not result in harm to herself or others. A hiccup does not take long to resolve. An example of a hiccup would be incorrectly ringing up an item at the store and having to apologize to a customer while she corrects her mistake. The customer is calm and kind during the interaction.

Level 2: Scrape

Phyllis calls a Level 2 problem a "scrape." A scrape is a situation that can be fixed without the assistance of others and does not result in harm to herself or others. However, a scrape takes longer to resolve than a hiccup and may involve stronger emotions in those around her.

She encountered a scrape two weeks ago when she had to drive through a construction zone on the way to work, couldn't find a parking space, and encountered an angry manager when she arrived thirty-five minutes after her shift started. Phyllis reminds herself that she was able to resolve this scrape by communicating with her manager and apologizing for being late. Even though a scrape feels more uncomfortable and distressing than a hiccup, no long-term harm is caused, and a scrape won't mean anything in another month.

Level 3: Yikes

Phyllis calls a level 3 problem a "yikes." She and her counselor have defined a "yikes" problem as one that requires some assistance from another person to fix and has consequences that last for a certain period, perhaps months. No one is physically harmed or endangered in a "yikes" problem.

Phyllis experienced a "yikes" problem last year at work. She had finished her training and was alone at the sales counter for the first time. An irate customer came in to complain about a problem with a product she had purchased, and Phyllis was unable to immediately reach a manager. Although Phyllis began by reassuring the customer that her concerns were important and would be attended to, the longer the customer ranted, the more upset Phyllis became. She eventually had a meltdown and yelled at the customer, telling her to calm down and wait for the manager.

Although this encounter caused no permanent harm, it was psychologically upsetting to everyone involved. Phyllis felt out of control and overwhelmed. The customer became more irate and filed a complaint with management. Phyllis was officially "coached" and monitored more closely for three months. She and her counselor developed coping strategies to use with angry customers. There was no lasting harm from the encounter, but it was stressful, it required the assistance of others, and the repercussions lasted a period of months.

Level 4: Perilous Pitfall

Phyllis encountered a "perilous pitfall" when it was discovered that the cracks in the drywall of her home were caused by problems in the foundation. A Level 4 problem requires significant help from others, a lengthy amount of time to resolve, and/or significant use of resources. A "perilous pitfall" also may have lasting consequences. Phyllis had no skill or knowledge in drywall repair and had to rely on multiple opinions from contractors and real estate specialists about how to correct the issues before her house would sell so she could move to a smaller space. She and her counselor worked on coping strategies for dealing with this long-lasting stress, such as breaking down large tasks into smaller tasks.

Level 5: Critical Emergency

Phyllis and her counselor discussed this final category of problem severity. This category is rarely experienced because it includes events that endanger the safety, health, and life of the individual or those around her. These problems often have consequences that are not fixable and that always require the assistance of others.

Phyllis has never encountered this level of emergency, but she has a cousin who was in the path of a tornado. His house was demolished, and his wife was injured so severely that her leg had to be amputated. Phyllis understands this level of problem is a critical emergency.

One of the benefits of using this problem severity scale was that Phyllis realized that most of her difficulties were hiccups or scrapes. Although she had encountered some "yikes" and "perilous pitfalls," these did not often occur. This helped Phyllis put in perspective the types of difficulties she dealt with on a regular basis.

Phyllis also liked having a way to label her problems. This provided structure and definition to something that felt threatening. When she was able to say, "Oh, this is just a hiccup," it decreased her fear response and helped her gain perspective. Additionally, she and her counselor developed coping strategies she could use at each problem level. When she encountered a hiccup, she knew she could apologize to the customer or coworker, take a deep breath, take a short walk around the store afterward to regroup, and squeeze a stress ball. Some strategies that helped her calm at a level 1 problem would not work at a level 3 problem because of the difference in intensity. She knew that with a level 3 problem, she might need to ask to be excused, to leave work early to regroup, or to take a meditation break.

Practice the Concepts Learned

1. Offer specifics when communicating

In this first practice exercise, you will use specifics rather than concepts in your conversations with the ASD individual. As discussed earlier in the chapter, he or she is likely to have trouble reading between the lines to accurately translate the speaker's message.

Consider the following example:

> Ashley came home from work and said to her ASD husband Mark, "I was swamped at work and had to bring stuff home. What a day!"

Although she was trying to let her husband know she needed rest and space to herself, Ashley's comment was open to interpretation.

To be more specific, she may have said something like this:

> "Things were so busy today that I've had to bring home some work to complete. I feel so overwhelmed. I won't be

able to chat with you, make dinner, or do other household chores. I don't even want to talk about my day. I just want to be alone so I can get my work done. If you could make dinner for us, that would be wonderful."

This second example contains many specifics about what Ashley can and cannot do at home that evening, as well as what she needs from Mark. It doesn't require him to "translate" her intended meaning, and therefore is more likely to be effective. Mark is able to cooperate by making dinner and doing more household tasks than he might typically do because he understands Ashley's needs.

Let's try some more examples:

An ASD individual may have trouble translating a statement such as, "Why are you so nosey about my personal business?"

Think of some ways to rewrite this scenario using specifics. There is no right or wrong answer, but some translation may be needed for the terms "nosey" and "personal business."

_____

_____

_____

_____

_____

_____

_____

Let's try a few more pretend scenarios before we practice additional concepts:

"I have to run to the store to get appetizers for our guests. Please clean up before I get home."

Think of some ways to rewrite this scenario using specifics:

_____

_____

_____

_____

_____

_____

Rewrite the following scenarios using more specifics:

"I need more freedom in our relationship."

_____

_____

_____

_____

_____

"Chill out! I can't get a word in edgewise."

_____

_____

_____

_____

_____

"I need that project organized so I can present it to the boss tomorrow."

_____

_____

_____

_____

"Calm down!"

_____

_____

_____

_____

_____

_____

_____

_____

_____

_____

2. Offer specific choices

In this exercise, various scenarios are presented using open-ended statements. In the space below each scenario, write a statement with more structure, less ambiguity, and fewer choices, and thus fewer decisions for the ASD individual to make.

To help you envision what this looks like, an example has been provided for you.

Example of an open-ended suggestion:

"Today is your birthday. We can do whatever you want to do! You get to choose."

Example of a suggestion with more structure and detail, less ambiguity, and fewer choices:

"We love to celebrate you on your birthday. Let's do something you love to do. I know you love to play role-playing games, and we could do that together. Or we could go out and see that new action-hero movie you're interested in. Do either of those sound good, or do you have another idea?"

Now you try some:

The teacher says, "Your assignment is to write a three-page single-spaced essay on what you did over the summer that impacted your views of human diversity."

_____

_____

_____

_____

_____

_____

A daughter speaks to her father about downsizing homes by saying, "Dad, I don't care where you start. Just do something to get this house under control. You have so much free time all day, every day. Just get something done."

_____

_____

_____

_____

_____

_____

Mom tells the family, "Melinda's graduation is this Sunday! We have a million things to do. We have to figure out who is coming, make sure we have enough seating, order food, and clean the house. Just start somewhere and help out!"

_____

_____

_____

_____

_____

_____

On a Friday night, a husband says to his ASD wife, "Let's do something relaxing tonight. You pick."

_____

_____

_____

_____

_____

_____

A coworker says, "We are having a potluck at work on Friday with a Hawaiian theme. What are you bringing?"

_____

_____

_____

_____

_____

_____

3. Offer additional time and space

Practice the concepts of providing time and/or space as a coping strategy for the ASD individual. A sample scenario is provided. Fill in the space below it with your own example.

Sample scenario #1:

Your ASD employee became agitated and yelled at a coworker when he was "pushed" to complete a project more quickly than he felt able to do.

Provide time: When you witness the escalation and shouting, you ask the coworker to return to his workstation, and you take the ASD individual aside to help him calm down. Once he is calmer, you ask him to walk around the block three times before coming back in to speak with you.

Provide space: You meet briefly with the ASD individual in your office. You are calm, encouraging, and clear. You let him know that his feelings and experiences at work are important, but that we can never have shouting at work. You ask him to meet with his counselor to work on a plan for dealing with his frustration in a different way the next time he encounters a stressful situation at work.

You know that his counseling appointment is in nine days, so you tell him that he can turn in his plan to you within two weeks. This offers him space because he can problem solve with the counselor outside of the work setting and write down the plan instead of speaking to you face to face.

Sample scenario #2:

In an attempt to help your grandfather Joe who is on the spectrum, you unclutter his living room while he is at a doctor's appointment with your mother. You throw away papers, napkins, and old food containers, and you do his laundry. Joe returns from the appointment and begins pacing and talking to himself when he sees the unexpected changes to his living space.

How can you build in time and space for Joe in the midst of this meltdown?

Provide time:

_____

_____

_____

_____

_____

_____

Provide space:

_____

_____

_____

_____

_____

_____

_____

4. Utilize rehearsal and social stories

Practice the concept of rehearsal by thinking of physical practice strategies and writing a social story. The following is an example:

Leonard is going to see a new primary care physician at the geriatric medical clinic. His caseworker knows that meeting new people and visiting new locations is stressful for Leonard. How can she utilize physical practice strategies before the appointment?

> Write a practice plan as if you are Leonard's caseworker. Your plan can utilize a picture of the doctor and nurse he will see that day, a map or visual representation of the building, a practice drive to see the building and to walk through the structure, and anything else you can think of to make this a concrete experience for Leonard ahead of time.

_____

_____

_____

_____

_____

_____

_____

_____

Next, write a social story for Leonard about his appointment. Your social story can incorporate the aspects of the practice plan described above, including an ending about expecting unexpected occurrences. These pictures and stories could be in a binder that Leonard looks through whenever he wants or needs to before the appointment, which is circled on his calendar.

_____
_____
_____
_____
_____
_____

5. Keep a record of unexpected occurrences

Jot down your thoughts, ideas, and plans about how this strategy may be useful for the individuals you have encountered on the spectrum. In what ways would making the unexpected expected help them manage the intensity of their daily lives?

_____
_____
_____
_____
_____

6. Make a schedule

Making a schedule involves being specific about aspects of an individual's routine that otherwise may be somewhat spontaneous. Scheduling these activities makes the day feel more structured and less ambiguous.

Think about an ASD individual you are helping, and create a hypothetical example of a schedule below. You may wish to include hygiene, meal times, connecting with others, work, school, or recreation.

_____

_____

_____

_____

_____

_____

7. Create rules and guidelines

Although the neurotypical individual may intuitively adjust to changes in life seasons by adapting his behavior, individuals in the spectrum may need specific cues, rules, and guidelines.

For example, rules may be created for an ASD individual who does not pay attention to hygiene and grooming. The rules may include a list of tasks that should be done and with what type of frequency.

Guidelines could be created regarding social behavior. For example, an ASD individual may be helped by the requirement that she not call or text someone more than twice without a reply.

What other real world or hypothetical rules and guidelines can you think of for an ASD individual?

_____

_____

_____

_____

_____

_____

8. How big is this problem?

An example of a rating scale was given in the chapter text for categorizing problems based on their impact and the stress level they cause, from a "hiccup" to a critical emergency. In the spaces below, develop your own rating scale and some coping strategies that might work at each level of intensity.

If you are working with an individual on the autism spectrum, have fun by allowing them to name each level in a way that is meaningful to them. Some terms to choose from may include the following: crisis, predicament, pinch, difficulty, crunch, bump in the road, scrape, disaster, pickle, or glitch. Other ASD individuals may wish to label each level with a visual image like a color or perhaps a movie or book character they think depicts that level of problem.

Remember, there is no right or wrong answer in labeling the levels; however, try to adhere to the definitions for each level provided in the chapter.

A Level 1 problem involves an unexpected event that is small, can be fixed without assistance, and does not result in harm to oneself or others.

We will call a Level 1 problem a _____

Give an example of a Level 1 problem:

_____

_____

_____

_____

_____

_____

_____

What coping strategies may work for an individual who is struggling with a Level 1 problem? For example, think of filling activities such as sensory inputs, special interests such as thinking about horses, or ways of creating distance and space such as taking a walk outside.

_____

_____

_____

_____

_____

A Level 2 problem is a situation that can be fixed without the assistance of others and does not result in harm to oneself or others. A Level 2 problem takes longer to resolve than a Level 1 problem and may involve stronger emotions in the people interacting with the individual.

We will call a Level 2 problem a _____

Give an example of a Level 2 problem:

_____

_____

_____

_____

_____

What coping strategies may work for an individual who is struggling with a Level 2 problem?

_____

_____

_____

_____

_____

_____

A Level 3 problem requires some assistance from another person to resolve and has consequences that last a certain period, perhaps months. No one is physically harmed or endangered in a Level 3 problem.

We will call a Level 3 problem a _____.

Give an example of a Level 3 problem:

_____

_____

_____

_____

_____

What coping strategies may work for an individual who is struggling with a Level 3 problem?

_____

_____

_____

_____

_____

A Level 4 problem requires significant help from others, a lengthy amount of time to resolve, and/or significant use of resources. A problem at this level may have lasting consequences.

We will call a Level 4 problem a _____.

Give an example of a Level 4 problem:

_____

_____

_____

_____

_____

What coping strategies may work for an individual who is struggling with a Level 4 problem?

_____

_____

_____

_____

_____

_____

A Level 5 problem is a rare occurrence that endangers the safety, health, and life of the individual or those around her. These problems often have consequences that are not fixable and that always require the assistance of others.

We will call a Level 5 problem a _____.

Give an example of a Level 5 problem:

_____

_____

_____

_____

_____

_____

What coping strategies may work for the individual at this level?

_____

_____

_____

_____

_____

_____

Chapter 7

Creating Momentum

As we noted in the Physics of Behavior chapter, some ASD individuals develop too much momentum toward a certain activity while others languish in a state of inertia. Although too much activity and over-reaction to the environment creates challenges for the ASD individual, I generally find that those who are under-reactive and sluggish tend to experience greater challenges. It often seems easier to teach people calming strategies than to prompt and/or motivate those who have very little internal drive.

The following examples illustrate individuals who have too much inertia (sluggishness) and not enough momentum:

- Seventy-two-year-old Marcia, who is known by her neighbors as a hoarder, keeps to herself and does not perform basic self-care or hygiene activities. She has not seen a doctor in over forty years.

- Twenty-six-year-old Tucker has a bachelor's degree in graphic design but has not felt energized to obtain or keep a job. He lives in his parents' basement where he watches YouTube videos and plays online role-playing games.

- Forty-three-year-old Benjamin accomplishes tasks at work without difficulty (the tasks are repetitive, predictable, and structured), but he does not initiate important tasks in the unstructured environment of his home where there is no external push to get things done.

Because individuals in the spectrum who are under-responsive to their environment do not have the internal drive or direction to accomplish tasks and take care of themselves adequately, they may require a consistent "push" from the environment to activate them in daily life. This constant demand on the environment to produce results can make improvement difficult because the environmental structure and demand needs to be provided by others—parents, family members, care workers, supervisors.

It is important to distinguish shutdown or withdrawal behaviors due to over-reaction to the environment because the environment feels too intense as opposed to behaviors that represent an under-reaction to the environment. In the first instance, someone could be withdrawn from others and never leave his room because he finds the world too intense to interact with—too loud, too unpredictable, too emotional.

In the second instance, the ASD individual could be withdrawn from others and never leave his room because he does not perceive the world as compelling enough for his participation or involvement in it. Instead he seems "in his own little world" and not appropriately aware of his environment, such as the lack of cleanliness in his apartment or the persistent pain that should prompt a visit to his doctor.

When helping an autistic individual who experiences persistent over-reaction to the environment, it's best to focus on calming behaviors as described in earlier chapters. It should also be noted that one can see behaviors of both types—over-reactive and under-reactive—in the same individual. A close analysis of the root cause of the individual's reactions is important to determine the best approach for managing daily life skills.

In general, I would suggest two types of intervention for the autistic individual who demonstrates behaviors rooted in under-reaction to the environment: sensory inputs to alert the nervous system and a structured environment with clear, attainable expectations and compelling rewards for accomplishment.

Sensory Inputs

As discussed in Chapter 5 of *Understanding Autism in Adults and Aging Adults 2nd Edition* sensory experiences during the day can increase alertness in someone who is feeling sluggish, and induce calm in someone who is feeling anxious or agitated. For the individual who experiences too much inertia, alerting and activating inputs are generally recommended. These inputs include experiences in the proprioceptive and the vestibular domain. Proprioceptive inputs include pushing, pulling, or hanging through the joints through whole body, jaw/mouth, or hand activities. Vestibular activities are those involving movement and balance that activate the inner ear. Examples include hanging upside down, swinging, or riding a bicycle through the neighborhood.

Examples of movement that do *not* activate the vestibular system include riding a stationary bike, lifting weights, or handling a fidget spinner. Although these examples involve movement of the hands, arms, and legs, they require no movement of the head, and thus the vestibular system is not activated.

Keep in mind that linear vestibular inputs—movement in one direction such as riding a bike, walking, or swimming—can be used at varying intensity levels depending on what the individual tolerates. I have some patients who seek roller coasters and zip lines for a more intense experience of linear vestibular input. Others cannot tolerate such intensity and will avoid movement in general. In those cases, a much more gentle vestibular input is suggested, such as rocking in a rocking chair or a rocking recliner, swinging in a hammock, or walking.

Some ASD individuals seek the intense alerting inputs of rotary vestibular input (circular movement such as spinning), but these individuals also tend to enjoy movement and do not have baseline inertia. Each individual is different, and the goal is to see what type, intensity, and frequency of inputs the person tolerates and benefits from.

Let's take the example of Linda, a nineteen-year-old ASD female with very low movement tolerance. She complains of dizziness and anxiety with the slightest movement and prefers to remain sedentary in her daily activities. She prefers to read books all day in her room rather than interact with others, and she forgets to attend to basic self-care activities such as hygiene and doing her laundry. Linda's inertia also hinders her progress in attaining independent life goals.

For Linda, the world of movement is intense, and staying still is preferable. Her behavioral inertia parallels her physical inertia. Her difficulties are somewhat circular in the sense that the more she avoids movement, the less proprioceptive and vestibular inputs she receives. This lack of input likely adds to her behavioral inertia.

Because of her movement intolerance, a physical program may include the following:

- Walking around the block three times a day in her neighborhood so the visual inputs are familiar.
- Reading while sitting on an exercise ball for fifteen minutes every two hours. The exercise ball provides pressure in the pelvic joints, allows for gentle movement of the body, and engages the core muscles of the body, which can help her feel more stable overall during movement activities.
- Doing the down dog yoga pose for inverted vestibular input (in this pose, the head is down) and for proprioceptive input into the arms and legs.

These joint and movement inputs are subtle and do not require extreme effort, but they move Linda's body more than what she typically experiences. The goal is to increase the joint and movement intensity and frequency over time to decrease some of her movement aversion and increase her tolerance for activating sensations.

Vincent is another example of an individual with a baseline of behavioral inertia. Unlike Linda, he tolerates movement well and in fact was very athletic in high school. However, he tends toward a sedentary lifestyle, perhaps in part because his special interest is online video gaming. He experiences a magnetic attraction to this activity all day every day unless he is prompted by others to engage in life outside his computer. Vincent benefits from having a schedule of athletic activities in spurts throughout the day, every day. For example, he takes a bike ride every morning, and he likes to swim or play tennis in the afternoon. Vincent needs this activating input to propel him to engage with others and make goal-oriented choices throughout the day.

Structure, Contingencies, and Rewards

The second factor in activating the ASD individual who has significant inertia is the creation of structure and motivating factors in the environment. This typically has to be done by family members or supportive individuals. Even if a plan for contingencies is developed during counseling sessions, success is often elusive if the plan is not activated and monitored by an individual in or near the home setting.

The good thing about setting up rewards for individuals with ASD is that they generally have hobbies or interests that are particularly compelling to them. One may have a fascination with maps, and another may enjoy collecting vintage superhero memorabilia. Whatever it is, the hobby or special interest can often be harnessed to provide motivation for the completion of other activities. For example, the individual may earn a new map or access to his maps after completion of specified tasks. Alternately, sometimes the incentive is outside of an individual's special interest.

Let's consider the example of Jeni, a twenty-three-year-old ASD individual with superior intellect and a history of good school performance in her structured high school environment. She struggled, however, in the less structured college environment, and dropped out of her mathematics degree program to return home. She has been living at her parents' house for the past three years without any sign of clear momentum toward independent living. She is lax in personal hygiene and reluctant to leave the house. Her needs are primarily met within the home setting. She spends much of her time on Pinterest and other websites where she looks at images that are primarily symmetric and angular in design, sometimes with color but usually black and white. She prints out these images and covers her bedroom walls with them.

Jeni has recently been interested in printing images of quilts because she loves the linear and angular features of certain quilt patterns, and the circles and spirals of others. The only outside contact she has with people is that which is scheduled by her parents. She prefers not to have these contacts, but she generally agrees in order to avoid conflict with her parents.

With the help of Jeni's parents to establish structure at home, Jeni and her counselor developed a plan that gradually increased the demand on her for independent living while providing opportunities for her to find reward.

Jeni was given a monetary goal per month based on a low "rent" amount of $150 plus money for utilities, food, and insurance, which totaled $300 at the start of the plan. Although this amount was not enough to cover her actual expenses, it was a good place to start so that she felt some pressure to show goal-oriented activity, but she was less likely to feel overwhelmed by this demand than she would if faced with real-world expenses.

Jeni and her parents made a list of activities she could perform during the month to earn deductions from her monthly bill of $300. These included exercise activities, family dinners, self-care tasks, and chores. She chose what to complete in order to (potentially) zero out her monthly balance and owe nothing to her parents.

Her parents understood that the goal was to see forward movement in Jeni's behavior. They realized that every goal would not be met, and the plan would only be effective with periodic adjustments. In fact, there was some up and down momentum, but over the course of a year, Jeni made significant improvements toward independence. The plan was adjusted several times to maintain an appropriate balance of comfort and challenge.

Jeni developed a routine of swimming and yoga that helped her maintain calm and a more activated state. She always had a baseline of inertia, but eventually found that the repetition of her exercise schedule gave her enough momentum to demonstrate more engagement in life.

Jeni was given a goal of getting a part-time job within three months of the plan's initiation. This goal was not met for various reasons including the job market and Jeni's perception that this goal felt more overwhelming than the others. However, her parents were able to adjust the goals so that she obtained two volunteer positions. One was two hours each weekend at a local church where she helped maintain the flowerbeds. She found that getting outside and performing this solitary activity helped her overall sense of vigor and well-being. The second began as a ten-hour weekly volunteer position at a local fabric store and increased to twenty hours per week within two months. Although the volunteer position did not pay her a salary, Jeni found she loved the environment and flourished around the fabrics and sewing projects. The staff began to show her the basics of sewing, and she could see that her love of symmetry and her mathematical background worked well with sewing. The final creations pleased her, and she looked forward to creating more. Her internet searches were now more focused on meaningful sewing projects than on eye-catching images to print out and put on the wall.

This volunteer position gave her a meaningful skill. In addition, she was eventually hired part-time and then full-time (thirty-two hours per week) with pay.

Jeni continued to seek significant alone time, but she developed a few friendly connections at the fabric store. She "filled up" when she returned home to her own room and looked at images on the computer or engaged in her exercise activities.

Her success in paying off her monthly debt to her parents was variable, but her counselor and parents maintained a strategy mindset that searched for solutions: Are there any barriers to the plan? Are the rewards compelling enough? Are the demands too high? They allowed some natural consequences that were appropriate to the context. For example, one month Jeni had an unpaid "rent" balance of $150. Her computer needed repairs, and she asked her parents to help her pay for the repairs so she could continue her internet searches. Her parents knew she needed to be able to look at images, but they told her she could get her computer fixed the next month if all her bills were paid. In the meantime, they made sure she had a wide variety of fabric sample books from the store to sort through. Although this did not give her the range of views that the internet provided, it gave her some outlet for her stress. She was able to manage this delay fairly well, and she completed enough tasks to get her computer fixed by the end of the next month.

Her parents understood that these things were challenging for Jeni, but they were pleased with her progress. Jeni could also see that she was making progress. This helped her self-esteem, and although not all goals were met as originally planned, the forward movement was maintained over time. After one year, she was still living in her parents' home, but she had a full-time job and was successfully completing self-care activities. The goal for the following year would be an independent living situation.

Practice the Concepts Learned

1. Sensory Inputs
Using proprioceptive and vestibular inputs can help the ASD individual improve alertness, attention, and energy toward daily activities. In practicing this concept, think about an individual in your life or consider a hypothetical example. What sensory inputs does the individual tolerate? Is there a balance of regular inputs that can help this person on the spectrum engage in daily activities and complete tasks with more consistency?

Make a list of activities that provide proprioceptive inputs. Remember, these are activities that put pressure in the joints. You may think of tasks that involve pulling, pushing, or hanging through the joints. A few examples are provided:

Lifting weights

Pulling weeds in the garden

Pull-up exercises

Rock climbing

_____

_____

_____

_____

_____

_____

_____

Make a list of activities that provide vestibular inputs. Remember, these activities involve movement and balance, and they specifically include movement of the head, which activates the inner ears. A few examples are provided:

Diving into a swimming pool

Jumping on a trampoline

Standing on a balance board while doing homework

Running

_____

_____

_____

_____

_____

In the section below, describe a possible schedule of inputs for the individual you are assisting. Keep in mind that the frequency and intensity of inputs throughout the day may change over time. For example, in kindergarten, a young student may benefit from ten-minute spurts of input every hour to successfully complete the school day and learn new material. In contrast, the same student in eighth grade may do well with a routine of running a mile before school, doing pull-ups for five minutes during lunch, and helping his dad in their landscaping business for thirty minutes after school (pushing hand mowers and pulling weeds).

_____

_____

_____

_____

_____

2. Structure, Contingencies, and Rewards

Some individuals in the spectrum rely on the environment to provide structure and momentum toward completing activities. When the environment does not provide an inherent "push," the individual may show a lack of engagement toward goals and self-care.

One strategy to build momentum toward goals is to create specific requirements and contingencies that may "simulate" independent living within the context of a monitored environment. Think of Jeni in this chapter and how her parents and counselor worked toward creating very clear goals and rewards to help her move toward age-appropriate independence.

Consider a hypothetical example or one involving the ASD individual in your life to help you develop a similar plan. Keep in mind the age of the individual. What would age-appropriate goals include? For example, goals for an eight-year-old may include brushing his teeth before bed, feeding the dog, and taking the trash out. Parents may develop a plan in which he can earn money for engaging in these activities, which he can spend on his preferred interests, such as purchasing a book about trains. Plans will differ in specifics depending on the age of the individual, the amount of daily living support, and the functional goals needed for the individual to improve in health and independence. Create an example below.

_____

_____

_____

_____

_____

_____

_____

_____

Final Thoughts

Successful Outcomes

*B*y joining me on the journey of learning about autistic behaviors and interventions, you have opened yourself to what may be a completely new way of looking at human behavior. I have invited you to consider the links between behavior and the brain, and to think about our human state with its limitations and its influence over our life outcomes. I am hopeful that this book has provided you with better understanding of behaviors in the autism spectrum, and has given you some practical strategies toward behavior improvement that you can implement with the ASD in your life to achieve successful outcomes for all.

If you have felt stuck in a rut of frustration or alone in your efforts to help the autistic individual who is dear to you, I hope this book provides some new ideas and forward momentum to give you a fresh start. When we fully understand that behavior is connected to brain functioning and not solely to motivation, character, and determination, we will truly be able to help every individual succeed according to his or her unique abilities.

A Note from the Author

$\mathcal{T}$hank you for taking the time to read this book to learn more about adults with autism spectrum disorder. I encourage you to recognize and support the strengths and challenges of all individuals in the autism spectrum, regardless of gender, age, or their unique patterns of behavior. When we fully understand that behavior is connected to brain functioning and not just to motivation, commitment, and determination, we will truly be able to help every individual succeed according to his or her abilities. All communities will benefit from improving the quality of life, physical health, relationships, and workplace independence for individuals within the autism spectrum. I invite you to join me in this endeavor.

Be sure to review this book and explore my other publications. Want to learn more? Check out my podcast and social media sites:

Podcast: Autism in the Adult
Facebook page: Autism in the Adult
Instagram @regan_autism
Twitter @regan_autism

My website, www.adultandgeriatricautism.com, includes resources for individuals on the autism spectrum and family members. Clinicians will find training courses and opportunities for professional consultation.

Thank you!
Theresa Regan PhD, CAS

CPSIA information can be obtained
at www.ICGtesting.com
Printed in the USA
BVHW031554251021
619812BV00001B/51